P9-CDB-438

WITHDRAWN

A12900 245242

ILLINOIS CENTRAL COLLEGE
PS662.B73
STACKS
Language and politics,

A12900 245242

PS
662   BROCKWAY
.B73   Language and politics

WITHDRAWN

A

LA
by

LA
by

WR
by

Illinois Central College
Learning Resource Center

USES OF ENGLISH

LANGUAGE
AND POLITICS
Selected Writing

Edited by

THOMAS P. BROCKWAY

BENNINGTON COLLEGE

Illinois Central College
Learning Resouce Center

D. C. HEATH AND COMPANY BOSTON

11690

PS
662
.B 73

LIBRARY OF CONGRESS CATALOG CARD NUMBER: 65-14110

Copyright © 1965 by D. C. Heath and Company

No part of the material covered by this copyright may be reproduced for any purpose without written permission of the publisher.

Printed in the United States of America

Printed March 1967

D. C. HEATH AND COMPANY

Boston   Englewood   Chicago   San Francisco
Atlanta   Dallas   London   Toronto

Contents

Introduction

This is a sampling of political discourse in the Western tradition. It is not a survey of political thought but rather an anthology to illustrate the diverse uses of language for political purposes. Selections from a few notable foreign works have been included in translation, but most of the authors and orators are English-speaking products of the 19th and 20th centuries. Included are almost as many politicians or statesmen as authors and journalists.

My modest hope for the volume is that it will basically change the reader's approach to political discourse, whether he is reading Rousseau, writing a term-paper, listening to campaign oratory, or participating directly in politics on the campus or beyond. The change should come about through a sharpened awareness of the nature and potential of rhetoric, more developed critical faculties, and greater appreciation of clarity, thrust and style in political expression.

Politics has been bleakly defined as the theory and practice of the art and science of government. Actually what gives politics its perennial fascination is the conflict and clash of ideas and ideologies, of candidates and interests, of regions and nations, to say nothing of constant tensions within politics itself. If one considers the roles of power and of principle in the political process, he finds an area of compatibility but also an area of antagonism in which compromise and even deception may flourish. It is this that has given politics its bad name even without Machiavelli's striking assist. But politics at its best or at its worst relies heavily on the language of persuasion, and it is in the careful analysis of political discourse, written or spoken, that we can best distinguish between the statesman and the demagogue.

How can this booklet be used in an English course? Some instructors will undoubtedly change the order, combine separated sections, omit, and add easily accessible outside reading. However, the opening essay, George Orwell's "Politics and the English Language," should be a serviceable introduction to any study of political writing and speech. The reader need not accept Orwell's scathing judgment of politics (he once said he had a horror of politics), and he may choose to re-work Orwell's standards of good writing; but the deeper he digs in Orwell, the greater reward will he find thereafter.

This might be followed by an intensive textual analysis of the short provocative chapter from Machiavelli. A few questions have been supplied for each selection, but the teacher may choose to frame questions which fit his own mode of analysis, and student questions are frequently searching and brilliantly illuminating.

The study of Machiavelli might be followed by examination of the selections from Plato, Adam Smith, Tocqueville, Lincoln. These would meet Orwell's exacting requirements for expressive prose, and would balance and offset his generous provision of horrible examples.

The topic of American oratory might be pursued from Webster to President Kennedy or Martin Luther King, or it could be limited to a comparative study of Senatorial discourse. Sir Winston Churchill's American mother brings his speech to Congress within earshot of American oratory and it might be analyzed at this point. Incidentally, scrutiny of Senator Beveridge's oration in support of Manifest Destiny should be followed by Finley Peter Dunne's delightful antidote, "Mr. Dooley on Taking the Philippines."

On such topics as freedom, democracy, civil rights, and peace, students could bring in any amount of contemporary material from books, periodicals and the press. While Congress is in session, the Congressional Record is a daily treasure house of oratory, denunciation, year-round electioneering, and an occasional great debate.

A great variety of assignments will occur to every teacher, from research in amplification of the brief headnotes, to the preparation of essays critical of, or orations in reply to, selections that deserve or invite such treatment. Obvious possibilities are comparisons of the content and style of any two Senators or of Lincoln's and Kennedy's inaugurals, re-writing one essay or speech in the style of another, or analysis of single texts by listing key words.

LANGUAGE AND POLITICS

I / The Language and Symbols of Politics

GEORGE ORWELL

Prose and Politics

This brilliant essay, "Politics and the English Language," gives the English writer, George Orwell, a claim to immortality quite apart from his *Animal Farm* and his jolting novel, *1984.** He wrote it at the end of World War II. Everything Orwell says here should be kept within mental reach as you read and reflect on later selections. George Orwell was the pseudonym of Eric Blair (1903–1950).

Most people who bother with the matter at all would admit that the English language is in a bad way, but it is generally assumed that we cannot by conscious action do anything about it. Our civilization is decadent and our language — so the argument runs — must inevitably share in the general collapse. It follows that any struggle against the abuse of language is a sentimental archaism, like preferring candles to electric light or hansom cabs to aeroplanes. Underneath this lies the half-conscious belief that language is a natural growth and not an instrument which we shape for our own purposes.

Now, it is clear that the decline of a language must ultimately have political and economic causes: it is not due simply to the bad influence of this or that individual writer. But an effect can become a cause, reinforcing the original cause and producing the same effect in an intensified form, and so on indefinitely. A man may take to drink because he feels

From George Orwell, *Shooting an Elephant and Other Essays* (N. Y. 1950) pp. 79–92. Copyright 1945, 1946, 1949, 1950 by Sonia Brownell Orwell. Reprinted by permission of Harcourt, Brace & World, Inc. and Martin Secker & Warburg. The essay first appeared in *Horizon*, a London literary magazine, and was reprinted in *The New Republic* in June, 1946.

himself to be a failure, and then fail all the more completely because he drinks. It is rather the same thing that is happening to the English language. It becomes ugly and inaccurate because our thoughts are foolish, but the slovenliness of our language makes it easier for us to have foolish thoughts. The point is that the process is reversible. Modern English, especially written English, is full of bad habits which spread by imitation and which can be avoided if one is willing to take the necessary trouble. If one gets rid of these habits one can think more clearly, and to think clearly is a necessary first step towards political regeneration: so that the fight against bad English is not frivolous and is not the exclusive concern of professional writers. I will come back to this presently, and I hope that by that time the meaning of what I have said here will have become clearer. Meanwhile, here are five specimens of the English language as it is now habitually written.

These five passages have not been picked out because they are especially bad — I could have quoted far worse if I had chosen — but because they illustrate various of the mental vices from which we now suffer. They are a little below the average, but are fairly representative samples. I number them so that I can refer back to them when necessary:

(1) I am not, indeed, sure whether it is not true to say that the Milton who once seemed not unlike a seventeenth-century Shelley had not become, out of an experience ever more bitter in each year, more alien [*sic*] to the founder of that Jesuit sect which nothing could induce him to tolerate.
PROFESSOR HAROLD LASKI (Essay in *Freedom of Expression*).

(2) Above all, we cannot play ducks and drakes with a native battery of idioms which prescribes such egregious collocations of vocables as the Basic *put up with* for *tolerate* or *put at a loss* for *bewilder*.
PROFESSOR LANCELOT HOGBEN (*Interglossa*).

(3) On the one side we have the free personality: by definition it is not neurotic, for it has neither conflict nor dream. Its desires, such as they are, are transparent, for they are just what institutional approval keeps in the forefront of consciousness; another institutional pattern would alter their number and intensity; there is little in them that is natural, irreducible, or culturally dangerous. But *on the other side,* the social bond itself is nothing but the mutual reflection of these self-secure integrities. Recall the definition of love. Is not this the very picture of a small academic? Where is there a place in this hall of mirrors for either personality or fraternity?
Essay on psychology in *Politics* (New York).

(4) All the "best people" from the gentlemen's clubs, and all the frantic fascist captains, united in common hatred of Socialism and bestial horror of the rising tide of the mass revolutionary movement, have turned to acts of

provocation, to foul incendiarism, to medieval legends of poisoned wells, to legalize their own destruction of proletarian organizations, and rouse the agitated petty-bourgeoisie to chauvinistic fervor on behalf of the fight against the revolutionary way out of the crisis.

Communist pamphlet.

(5) If a new spirit *is* to be infused into this old country, there is one thorny and contentious reform which must be tackled, and that is the humanization and galvanization of the B.B.C. Timidity here will bespeak canker and atrophy of the soul. The heart of Britain may be sound and of strong beat, for instance, but the British lion's roar at present is like that of Bottom in Shakespeare's *Midsummer Night's Dream* — as gentle as any sucking dove. A virile new Britain cannot continue indefinitely to be traduced in the eyes or rather ears, of the world by the effete languors of Langham Place, brazenly masquerading as "standard English." When the Voice of Britain is heard at nine o'clock, better far and infinitely less ludicrous to hear aitches honestly dropped than the present priggish, inflated, inhibited, school-ma'amish arch braying of blameless bashful mewing maidens!

Letter in *Tribune*

Each of these passages has faults of its own, but, quite apart from avoidable ugliness, two qualities are common to all of them. The first is staleness of imagery; the other is lack of precision. The writer either has a meaning and cannot express it, or he inadvertently says something else, or he is almost indifferent as to whether his words mean anything or not. This mixture of vagueness and sheer incompetence is the most marked characteristic of modern English prose, and especially of any kind of political writing. As soon as certain topics are raised, the concrete melts into the abstract and no one seems able to think of turns of speech that are not hackneyed: prose consists less and less of *words* chosen for the sake of their meaning, and more and more of *phrases* tacked together like the sections of a prefabricated hen-house. I list below, with notes and examples, various of the tricks by means of which the work of prose-construction is habitually dodged:

Dying metaphors. A newly invented metaphor assists thought by evoking a visual image, while on the other hand a metaphor which is technically "dead" (e.g. *iron resolution*) has in effect reverted to being an ordinary word and can generally be used without loss of vividness. But in between these two classes there is a huge dump of worn-out metaphors which have lost all evocative power and are merely used because they save people the trouble of inventing phrases for themselves. Examples are: *Ring the changes on, take up the cudgels for, toe the line, ride roughshod over, stand shoulder to shoulder with, play into the hands of, no axe to grind, grist to the mill, fishing in troubled waters, on the order of the day, Achilles' heel, swan song, hotbed.* Many of these are used without knowledge of their meaning (what is a "rift," for instance?), and incompatible metaphors are frequently mixed, a sure sign that the writer is not interested in what he is saying. . . .

Operators or *verbal false limbs.* These save the trouble of picking out appropriate verbs and nouns, and at the same time pad each sentence with extra syllables which give it an appearance of symmetry. Characteristic phrases are *render inoperative, militate against, make contact with, be subjected to, give rise to, give grounds for, have the effect of, play a leading part (role) in, make itself felt, take effect, exhibit a tendency to, serve the purpose of, etc., etc.* The keynote is the elimination of simple verbs. Instead of being a single word, such as *break, stop, spoil, mend, kill,* a verb becomes a *phrase,* made up of a noun or adjective tacked on to some general-purposes verb such as *prove, serve, form, play, render.* In addition, the passive voice is wherever possible used in preference to the active, and noun constructions are used instead of gerunds (*by examination of* instead of *by examining*). The range of verbs is further cut down by means of the *-ize* and *de-* formations, and the banal statements are given an appearance of profundity by means of the *not un-* formation. Simple conjunctions and prepositions are replaced by such phrases as *with respect to, having regard to, the fact that, by dint of, in view of, in the interests of, on the hypothesis that;* and the ends of sentences are saved by anticlimax by such resounding common-places as *greatly to be desired, cannot be left out of account, a development to be expected in the near future, deserving of serious consideration, brought to a satisfactory conclusion,* and so on and so forth.

Pretentious diction. Words like *phenomenon, element, individual* (as noun), *objective, categorical, effective, virtual, basic, primary, promote, constitute, exhibit, exploit, utilize, eliminate, liquidate,* are used to dress up simple statement and give an air of scientific impartiality to biased judgments. Adjectives like *epoch-making, epic, historic, unforgettable, triumphant, age-old, inevitable, inexorable, veritable,* are used to dignify the sordid processes of international politics, while writing that aims at glorifying war usually takes on an archaic color, its characteristic words being: *realm, throne, chariot, mailed fist, trident, sword, shield, buckler, banner, jackboot, clarion.* Foreign words and expressions such as *cul de sac, ancien régime, deus ex machina, mutatis mutandis, status quo, gleichschaltung, weltanschauung,* are used to give an air of culture and elegance. Except for the useful abbreviations *i.e., e.g.,* and *etc.,* there is no real need for any of the hundreds of foreign phrases now current in English. Bad writers, and especially scientific, political and sociological writers are nearly always haunted by the notion that Latin or Greek words are grander than Saxon ones, and unnecessary words like *expedite, ameliorate, predict, extraneous, deracinated, clandestine, subaqueous* and hundreds of others constantly gain ground from their Anglo-Saxon opposite numbers. . . .

Meaningless words. In certain kinds of writing, particularly in art criticism and literary criticism, it is normal to come across long passages which are almost completely lacking in meaning. Words like *romantic, plastic, values, human, dead, sentimental, natural, vitality,* as used in art criticism, are strictly meaningless, in the sense that they not only do not point to any discoverable object, but are hardly ever expected to do so by the reader. . . . Many political words are similarly abused. The word *Fascism* has now no meaning except in so far as it signifies "something not desirable." The words *democracy, socialism, freedom, patriotic, realistic, justice,* have each of them several different meanings which cannot be reconciled with one another. In the case of a word like *democracy,* not only is there no agreed definition, but the attempt to make one is resisted from all sides. It is almost universally felt that when we call a country democratic we are praising it: consequently the defenders of every kind of régime claim that it is a democracy, and fear that they might have to stop using the word if it were tied down to any one meaning. . . .

Now that I have made this catalogue of swindles and perversions, let me give another example of the kind of writing that they lead to. This time it must of its nature be an imaginary one. I am going to translate a passage of good English into modern English of the worst sort. Here is a well-known verse from *Ecclesiastes:*

"I returned and saw under the sun, that the race is not to the swift, nor the battle to the strong, neither yet bread to the wise, nor yet riches to men of understanding, nor yet favour to men of skill; but time and chance happeneth to them all."

Here it is in modern English:

"Objective consideration of contemporary phenomena compels the conclusion that success or failure in competitive activities exhibits no tendency to be commensurate with innate capacity, but that a considerable element of the unpredictable must invariably be taken into account."

This is a parody, but not a very gross one. Exhibit (3), above, for instance, contains several patches of the same kind of English. It will be seen that I have not made a full translation. The beginning and ending of the sentence follow the original meaning fairly closely, but in the middle the concrete illustrations — race, battle, bread — dissolve into the vague phrase "success or failure in competitive activities." This had to be so, because no modern writer of the kind I am discussing — no one capable of using phrases like "objective consideration of contemporary phenomena" — would ever tabulate his thoughts in that precise and detailed way. The whole tendency of modern prose is away from concreteness. Now analyse these two sentences a little more closely. The first contains forty-nine words but only sixty syllables, and all its words are those of everyday life. The second contains thirty-eight words of ninety syllables: eighteen of its words are from Latin roots, and one from Greek. The first sentence contains six vivid images, and only one phrase ("time and chance") that could be called vague. The second contains not a single fresh, arresting phrase, and in spite of its ninety syllables it gives only a shortened version of the meaning contained in the first. Yet without a doubt it is the second kind of sentence that is gaining ground in modern English. I do not want to exaggerate. This kind of writing is not yet universal, and outcrops of simplicity will occur here and there in the worst-written page. Still, if you or I were told to write a few lines on the uncertainty of human fortunes, we should probably come much nearer to my imaginary sentence than to the one from *Ecclesiastes*.

As I have tried to show, modern writing at its worst does not consist in picking out words for the sake of their meaning and inventing images in order to make the meaning clearer. It consists in gumming together long strips of words which have already been set in order by someone else, and making the results presentable by sheer humbug. The attraction of this way of writing is that it is easy. It is easier — even quicker, once you have the habit — to say *In my opinion it is not an unjustifiable assumption that* than to say *I think*. If you use ready-made phrases, you not only don't have to hunt about for words; you also don't have to bother with the rhythms of your sentences, since these phrases are generally so arranged as to be more or less euphonious. When you are composing in a hurry — when you are dictating to a stenographer, for instance, or making a public speech — it is natural to fall into a pretentious, Latinized style. Tags like *a consideration which we should do well to bear in mind* or *a conclusion to which all of us would readily assent* will save many a sentence from coming down with a bump. By using stale metaphors, similes and idioms, you save much mental effort, at the cost of leaving your meaning vague, not only for your reader but for yourself. This is the significance of mixed metaphors. The sole aim of a metaphor is to call up a visual image. When these images clash — as in *The Fascist octopus has sung its swan song, the jackboot is thrown into the melting pot* — it can be taken as certain that the writer is not seeing a mental image of the objects he is naming; in other words he is not really thinking. Look again at the examples I gave at the beginning of this essay. Professor Laski (1) uses five negatives in fifty-three words. One of these is superfluous, making nonsense of the whole passage, and in addition there is the slip *alien* for akin, making further nonsense, and several avoidable pieces of clumsiness which increase the general vagueness. Professor Hogben (2) plays ducks and drakes with a battery which is able to write prescriptions, and, while disapproving of the everyday phrase *put up with,* is unwilling to look *egregious* up in the dictionary and see what it means; (3), if one takes an uncharitable attitude towards it, is simply meaningless: probably one could work out its intended meaning by reading the whole of the article in which it occurs. In (4), the writer knows more or less what he wants to say, but an accumulation of stale phrases chokes him like tea leaves blocking a sink. In (5), words and meaning have almost parted company. People who write in this manner usually have a general emotional meaning — they dislike one thing and want to express solidarity with another — but they are not interested in the detail of what they are saying. A scrupulous writer, in every sentence that he writes, will ask himself at least four questions, thus: What am I trying to say? What words will express it? What image or idiom will make it clearer? Is this image fresh enough to have an effect? And he will probably ask himself two more: Could I put it more shortly? Have I said anything that is avoidably ugly? But you are not obliged to go to all this trouble. You can shirk it by simply throwing your mind open and letting the ready-made phrases come crowding in. They will construct your sentences for you — even think your thoughts for you, to a certain extent — and at need they will perform the important service of partially concealing your meaning even from yourself. It is at this point that the special connection between politics and the debasement of language becomes clear.

In our time it is broadly true that political writing is bad writing. Where it is not true, it will generally be found that the writer is some kind of rebel, expressing his private opinions and not a "party line." Orthodoxy, of whatever color, seems to demand a lifeless, imitative style. The political dialects to be found in pamphlets, leading articles, manifestos, White Papers and the speeches of under-secretaries do, of course, vary from party to party, but they are all alike in that one almost never finds in them a fresh, vivid, home-made turn of speech. When one watches some tired hack on the platform mechanically repeating the familiar phrases — *bestial atrocities, iron heel, bloodstained tyranny, free peoples of the world, stand shoulder to shoulder* — one often has a curious feeling that one is not watching a live human being but some kind of dummy: a feeling which suddenly becomes stronger at moments when the light catches the speaker's spectacles and turns them into blank discs which seem to have no eyes behind them. And this is not altogether fanciful. A speaker who uses that kind of phraseology has gone some distance towards turning himself into a machine. The appropriate noises are coming out of his larynx, but his brain is not involved as it would be if he were choosing his words for himself. If the speech he is making is one that he is accustomed to make over and over again, he may be almost unconscious of what he is saying, as one is when one utters the responses in church. And this reduced state of consciousness, if not indispensable, is at any rate favorable to political conformity.

In our time, political speech and writing are largely the defence of the indefensible. Things like the continuance of British rule in India, the Russian purges and deportations, the dropping of the atom bombs on Japan, can indeed be defended, but only by arguments which are too brutal for most people to face, and which do not square with the professed aims of political parties. Thus political language has to consist largely of euphemism, question-begging and sheer cloudy vagueness. Defenceless villages are bombarded from the air, the inhabitants driven out into the countryside, the cattle machine-gunned, the huts set on fire with incendiary bullets: this is called *pacification*. Millions of peasants are robbed of their farms and sent trudging along the roads with no more than they can carry: this is called *transfer of population* or *rectification of frontiers*. People are imprisoned for years without trial, or shot in the back of the neck or sent to die of scurvy in Arctic lumber camps: this is called *elimination of unreliable elements*. Such phraseology is needed if one wants to name things without calling up mental pictures of them. Consider for instance some comfortable English professor defending Russian totalitarianism. He cannot say outright, "I believe in killing off your opponents when you can get good results by doing so." Probably, therefore, he will say something like this:

"While freely conceding that the Soviet régime exhibits certain features which the humanitarian may be inclined to deplore, we must, I think, agree that a certain curtailment of the right to political opposition is an unavoidable concomitant of transitional periods, and that the rigors which the Russian people have been called upon to undergo have been amply justified in the sphere of concrete achievement."

The inflated style is itself a kind of euphemism. A mass of Latin words falls upon the facts like soft snow, blurring the outlines and covering up all the details. The great enemy of clear language is insincerity. When there is a gap between one's real and one's declared aims, one turns as it were instinctively to long words and exhausted idioms, like a cuttlefish squirting out ink. In our age there is no such thing as "keeping out of politics." All issues are political issues, and politics itself is a mass of lies, evasions, folly, hatred and schizophrenia. When the general atmosphere is bad, language must suffer. I should expect to find — this is a guess which I have not sufficient knowledge to verify — that the German, Russian and Italian languages have all deteriorated in the last ten or fifteen years, as a result of dictatorship.

But if thought corrupts language, language can also corrupt thought. A bad usage can spread by tradition and imitation, even among people who should and do know better. The debased language that I have been discussing is in some ways very convenient. Phrases like *a not unjustifiable assumption, leaves much to be desired, would serve no good purpose, a consideration which we should do well to bear in mind*, are a continuous temptation, a packet of aspirins always at one's elbow. Look back through this essay, and for certain you will find that I have again and again committed the very faults I am protesting against.

I said earlier that the decadence of our language is probably curable. Those who deny this would argue, if they produced an argument at all, that language merely reflects existing social conditions, and that we cannot influence its development by any direct tinkering with words and constructions. So far as the general tone or spirit of a language goes, this may be true, but it is not true in detail. Silly words and expressions have often disappeared, not through any evolutionary process but owing to the conscious action of a minority. Two recent examples were *explore every avenue* and *leave no stone unturned,* which were killed by the jeers of a few journalists. There is a long list of flyblown metaphors which could similarly be got rid of if enough people would interest themselves in the job; and it should also be possible to laugh the *not un-* formation out of existence,[1] to reduce the amount of Latin and Greek in the average sentence, to drive out foreign phrases and strayed scientific words, and, in general, to make pretentiousness unfashionable. But all these are minor points. The defence of the English language implies more than this, and perhaps it is best to start by saying what it does *not* imply.

To begin with it has nothing to do with archaism, with the salvaging of obsolete words and turns of speech, or with the setting up of a "standard English" which must never be departed from. On the contrary, it is especially concerned with the scrapping of every word or idiom which has outworn its usefulness. It has nothing to do with correct grammar and syntax, which are of no importance so long as one makes one's meaning clear, or with the avoidance of Americanisms, or with having what is called a "good prose style." On the other hand it is not concerned with fake simplicity and the attempt to make written English colloquial. Nor does it even imply in every case preferring the Saxon word to the Latin one, though it does imply using the fewest and shortest words that will cover one's meaning. What is above all needed is to let the meaning choose

[1] One can cure oneself of the *not un-* formation by memorizing this sentence: *A not unblack dog was chasing a not unsmall rabbit across a not ungreen field.*

the word, and not the other way about. In prose, the worst thing one can do with words is to surrender to them. When you think of a concrete object, you think wordlessly, and then, if you want to describe the thing you have been visualizing you probably hunt about till you find the exact words that seem to fit it. When you think of something abstract you are more inclined to use words from the start, and unless you make a conscious effort to prevent it, the existing dialect will come rushing in and do the job for you, at the expense of blurring or even changing your meaning. Probably it is better to put off using words as long as possible and get one's meaning as clear as one can through pictures or sensations. Afterwards one can choose — not simply *accept* — the phrases that will best cover the meaning, and then switch round and decide what impression one's words are likely to make on another person. This last effort of the mind cuts out all stale or mixed images, all prefabricated phrases, needless repetitions, and humbug and vagueness generally. But one can often be in doubt about the effect of a word or a phrase, and one needs rules that one can rely on when instinct fails. I think the following rules will cover most cases:

(i) Never use a metaphor, simile or other figure of speech which you are used to seeing in print.

(ii) Never use a long word where a short one will do.

(iii) If it is possible to cut a word out, always cut it out.

(iv) Never use the passive where you can use the active.

(v) Never use a foreign phrase, a scientific word or a jargon word if you can think of an everyday English equivalent.

(vi) Break any of these rules sooner than say anything outright barbarous.

These rules sound elementary, and so they are, but they demand a deep change of attitude in anyone who has grown used to writing in the style now fashionable. One could keep all of them and still write bad English, but one could not write the kind of stuff that I quoted in those five specimens at the beginning of this article.

I have not here been considering the literary use of language, but merely language as an instrument for expressing and not for concealing or preventing thought. Stuart Chase and others have come near to claiming that all abstract words are meaningless, and have used this as a pretext for advocating a kind of political quietism. Since you don't know what Fascism is, how can you struggle against Fascism? One need not swallow such absurdities as this, but one ought to recognize that the present political chaos is connected with the decay of language, and that one can probably bring about some improvement by starting at the verbal end. If you simplify your English, you are freed from the worst follies of orthodoxy. You cannot speak any of the necessary dialects, and when you make a stupid remark its stupidity will be obvious, even to yourself. Political language — and with variations this is true of all political parties, from Conservatives to Anarchists — is designed to make lies sound truthful and murder respectable, and to give an appearance of solidity to pure wind. One cannot change this all in a moment, but one can at least change one's own habits, and from time to time one can even, if one jeers loudly enough, send some worn-out and useless phrase — some *jackboot, Achilles' heel, hotbed, melting pot, acid test, veritable inferno* or other lump of verbal refuse — into the dustbin where it belongs.

NICCOLÒ MACHIAVELLI

Principles and Politics

George Orwell's essay gives examples of writing which range from bad to shocking. In contrast here is a selection from Machiavelli which meets Orwell's standard of simple, expressive language. Niccolò Machiavelli (1469–1527) was a Florentine statesman and writer who experienced imprisonment, exile and fame. We borrow a chapter, "How Princes should keep faith," from *The Prince.** Written in 1513 this book made Machiavellian a synonym for unprincipled state-craft.

How Princes should keep faith

Every one recognises how praiseworthy it is in a Prince to keep faith, and to act uprightly and not craftily. Nevertheless, we see from what has happened in our own days that Princes who have set little store by their word, but have known how to over-reach others by their cunning, have accomplished great things, and in the end had the better of those who trusted to honest dealing.

Be it known, then, that there are two ways of contending, one in accordance with the laws, the other by force; the first of which is proper to men, the second to beasts. But since the first method is often ineffectual, it becomes necessary to resort to the second. A Prince should, therefore, understand how to use well both the man and the beast. And this lesson has been covertly taught by the ancient writers, who relate how Achilles and many others of these old Princes were given over to be brought up and trained by Chiron the Centaur; since the only meaning of their having

* From Machiavelli, *The Prince,* Trans. by N. H. Hill (Oxford, 1913) pp. 125–30. By permission of the Oxford University Press.

for teacher one who was half man and half beast is, that it is necessary for a Prince to know how to use both natures, and that the one without the other has no stability.

But since a Prince should know how to use the beast's nature wisely, he ought of beasts to choose both the lion and the fox; for the lion cannot guard himself from the toils, nor the fox from wolves. He must therefore be a fox to discern toils, and a lion to drive off wolves.

To rely wholly on the lion is unwise; and for this reason a prudent Prince neither can nor ought to keep his word when to keep it is hurtful to him and the causes which led him to pledge it are removed. If all men were good, this would not be good advice, but since they are dishonest and do not keep faith with you, you, in return, need not keep faith with them; and no Prince was ever at a loss for plausible reasons to cloak a breach of faith. Of this numberless recent instances could be given, and it might be shown how many solemn treaties and engagements have been rendered inoperative and idle through want of faith in Princes, and that he who has best known to play the fox has had the best success.

It is necessary, indeed, to put a good colour on this nature, and to be skilful in feigning and dissembling. But men are so simple, and governed so absolutely by their present needs, that he who wishes to deceive will never fail in finding willing dupes. One recent example I will not omit. Pope Alexander VI had no care or thought but how to deceive, and always found material to work on. No man ever had a more effective manner of asseverating, or made promises with more solemn protestations, or observed them less. And yet, because he understood this side of human nature, his frauds always succeeded.

It is not essential, then, that a Prince should have all the good qualities I have enumerated above, but it is most essential that he should seem to have them. Nay, I will venture to affirm that if he has and invariably practises them all, they are hurtful, whereas the appearance of having them is useful. Thus, it is well to seem merciful, faithful, humane, religious, and upright, and also to be so; but the mind should remain so balanced that were it needful not to be so, you should be able and know how to change to the contrary.

And you are to understand that a Prince, and most of all a new Prince, cannot observe all those rules of conduct in respect whereof men are accounted good, being often forced, in order to preserve his Princedom, to act in opposition to good faith, charity, humanity, and religion. He must therefore keep his mind ready to shift as the winds and tides of Fortune turn, and, as I have already said, ought not to quit good courses if he can help it, but should know how to follow evil if he must.

A Prince should therefore be very careful that nothing ever escapes his lips which is not replete with the five qualities above named, so that to see and hear him, one would think him the embodiment of mercy, good faith, integrity, kindliness, and religion. And there is no virtue which it is more necessary for him to seem to possess than this last; because men in general judge rather by the eye than by the hand, for all can see but few can touch. Every one sees what you seem, but few know what you are, and these few dare not oppose themselves to the opinion of the many who have the majesty of the State to back them up.

Moreover, in the actions of all men, and most of all of Princes, where there is no tribunal to which we can appeal, we look to results. Wherefore if a Prince succeeds in establishing and maintaining his authority, the means will always be judged honourable and be approved by every one. For the vulgar are always taken by appearances and by results, and the world is made up of the vulgar, the few only finding room when the many have no longer ground to stand on.

A certain Prince of our own days, whom it is as well not to name, is always preaching peace and good faith, although the mortal enemy of both; and both, had he practised as he preaches, would, oftener than once, have lost him his kingdom and authority.

HAROLD LASSWELL

Symbols in Political Manipulation

Harold Dwight Lasswell was born in Illinois in 1902, and educated at the University of Chicago where he taught for some years. He is now Professor of Law and Political Science in the Yale Law School. Professor Lasswell was a pioneer in utilizing psychology in political analysis. This selection appears in a chapter entitled "Symbols" in *Politics, Who Gets What, When, How*, written in 1936.*

Any elite defends and asserts itself in the name of symbols of the common destiny. Such symbols are the "ideology" of the established order, the "utopia" of counter-elites. By the use of sanctioned words and gestures the elite elicits blood, work, taxes, applause, from the masses. When the political order works smoothly, the masses venerate the symbols; the elite, self-righteous and unafraid, suffers from no withering sense of immorality. "God's in his heaven — all's right with the world." "In union there is strength" — not exploitation.

A well-established ideology perpetuates itself with little planned propaganda by those whom it benefits most. When thought is taken about

* Reprinted with permission of the publisher from *Politics, Who Gets What, When, How* by Harold Lasswell. Copyright 1951 by The Free Press, a corporation.

ways and means of sowing conviction, conviction has already languished, the basic outlook of society has decayed, or a new, triumphant outlook has not yet gripped the automatic loyalties of old and young. Happy indeed is the nation that has no thought of itself; or happy at least are the few who procure the principal benefits of universal acquiescence. Systems of life which confer special benefits on the other fellow need fear no plots or conspiracies when the masses are moved by faith and the elites are inspired by self-confidence.

Any well-knit way of life molds human behavior into its own design. The individualism of bourgeois society like the communism of a socialized state must be inculcated from the nursery to the grave. In the United States, as one among the bourgeois nations, the life of personal achievement and personal responsibility is extolled in song and story from the very beginning of consciousness. Penny banks instill the habit of thrift; trading in the schoolyard propagates the bourgeois scale of values. Individual marks at school set the person at rivalrous odds with his fellows. "Success and failure depend on you." "Strive and succeed" means "If you strive, success comes; if success does not come, you have not striven hard enough." . . .

The emblems and words of the organized community are also part of the precious haze of early experience. In the United States the memories of all are entwined with the flag, snapping in the breeze on Memorial Day; "The Star-Spangled Banner," sung in uncertain unison on special holidays; the oath of allegiance to the flag. . . . On occasions like the inauguration of the President, the unifying symbols of the nation rise again to the threshold of attention. . . . Inaugural oratory has invariably contained reference to the deity, and usually to words like "freedom," "liberty," "independence," "economy," "self-government." Even George Washington made an allusion to the common past. . . . Usually there were self-adulatory words like "intelligence of our people, our righteous people, our great nation."

In the picture language of the public, reflected in cartoons, foreign nations have often played a sorry role, except when public sympathy moved more or less episodically in their favor. For many years the "Mexican" stereotype included a bolero coat, a large sombrero, spurs, revolver, and rifle. The clothes were often torn and ragged, with patched shoes or bare feet. The dark hair, slightly upturned mustache, dark eyes, clenched fist, defiant face aroused annoyance rather than hatred. The "Mexican" was often shown as a small, thin urchin who should be soundly spanked and put to bed. Sometimes he was depicted as playing with fire, or sticking his tongue out at Uncle Sam, or being caught in a juvenile prank by his policeman neighbor to the north. . . .

The bias against government is strikingly indicated by the absence of a cartoon stereotype for the public as a recipient of benefits from public expenditures. The emphasis is all on the "Taxpayer." Often arrayed in a dark suit with a white collar, four-in-hand tie, sometimes with a white vest, often with light trousers, the taxpayer is one of those pathetic souls who always get it in the neck. . . . He may be an Isaac about to be sacrificed; a bandaged cripple leaving the office of Doc. Democrat to get relief from Doc. G. O. P.; a rower, trying to row five large cruisers to the scrap heap; a sawhorse, on which governmental extravagances and waste are teeter-tottering.

When elites resort to propaganda, the tactical problem is to select symbols and channels capable of eliciting the desired concerted acts. There is incessant resort to repetition or distraction. The changing emotional requirements of the community, moods of submissiveness, moods of self-assertion, all complicate the task of managing men in the mass. . . . Propaganda, when successful, is astute in handling: Aggressiveness, Guilt, Weakness, Affection.

The organization of the community for war takes advantage of the concentrated aggressiveness which accumulates in any crisis. . . . Hostile impulses arouse guilt feelings because society has taught the individual during infancy, childhood, and juvenility to chasten his rages. The initial tendency to hold the destructive tendencies in check by raging against the self can be dealt with by projecting the accusation away from the self and raging at the "immorality" of the enemy. . . .

As crisis grows, the "nation" is constantly kept at the focus of attention. The recurring preoccupations of everyday life are modified by news and rumors of international friction. All eyes focus upon the fate of the national "we" symbol in relation to the surrounding "they" symbols. Love and respect for the symbols of the foreigner are withdrawn and become attached to symbols of the collective "we." The sense of being threatened increases the need for love; hence the symbol of the nation is redefined as infinitely protective and indulgent, powerful and wise. . . .

The object of revolution, like war, is to attain coercive predominance over the enemy as a means of working one's will with him. Revolutionary propaganda selects symbols which are calculated to detach the affections of the masses from the existing symbols of authority, to attach these affections to challenging symbols, and to direct hostilities toward existing symbols of authority. This is infinitely more complex than the psychological problem of war propaganda [since] the great revolutions are in defiance of emotions which have been directed by nurses, teachers, guardians, and parents along "accredited" channels of expression. Revolutions are ruptures of conscience. . . .

Partial revolutionary movements are led by an elite which fights to exterminate those who are associated with the latest world revolutionary movement. Such movements, like Italian Fascism and German National Socialism, are belligerently anti-alien and pro-national. Regardless of how much they borrow in symbol or practice from the latest world revolutionary pattern, they conceal the theft, abominate the source.

The use of the "non-Aryan" as the unifying devil behind all the lesser devils of Marxism, Versailles, Weimar, Dawes Plan, is easy to understand. The same type of mass movement in Italy had not utilized the Jew; but several circumstances conspired to heighten the availability of the Jew as a target of demagoguery in Germany. . . . There were few Jews in Germany: they were bankers, merchants, and professional people who were inclined to treat Jew-baiting with disdain. There was no proletarian bloc of Jews to create a pro-Jewish backfire among the working masses. In short, the Jews were so numerous that they could conveniently be hated; not so numerous that they could effectively retaliate. The solid background of traditional anti-Semitism could be retouched and exploited with impunity.

Anti-Semitism gave an opportunity to discharge hatred against the rich and successful without espousing the proletarian socialists. Not "capitalism" but "Jewish profiteering" was the festering sore. . . . Even middle-class hatred of the proletarian could be split by means of the Jewish symbol. Thus the workers who were sufficiently German to renounce "Jewish doctrine" could be tolerated; those who remained Jewish and "Red" and "Marxist" could be destroyed.

Aristocratic hatred of the consequences of modern industrialism could be split by having recourse to the Jew. The undesirable features exhibited the effect of international Jewish finance, not the inherent traits of the system. Hence it became possible to cooperate with capitalistic elements, and to turn the rage generated by recent economic changes against the irrelevant scapegoat. . . .

Anti-Semitism was also an important means of discharging the hatred of the villager against the urbanite. . . . City types are prominent among the enemies of the mores, and the Jews were city types. . . . The stresses of war, blockade, inflation, and deflation had exacted a tremendous moral toll in Germany. Multitudes had succumbed to sexual and property "temptations"; hence they were predisposed toward "purification" to remove the heavy hand of conscience. For them the Jew was the sacrificial Isaac. Indeed, the whole nineteenth century had witnessed the growth of the secular cult of nationalism, furnishing a substitute for the fading appeal of established religion. This decline of piety, however, left legacies of guilt which could be expiated by attacking the Jew, traditional enemy of Christianity.

Plainly the Jew was available as the symbol which more than any other could be utilized as a target of irrelevant emotional drives. The hatred of the country for the city, of the aristocracy for the plutocracy, of the middle class for the manual toilers and the aristocracy and the plutocracy could be displaced upon the Jew. The frustrations of economic adversity and international humiliation, guilt from immorality, guilt from diminishing piety — these stresses within the lives of Germans were available to be exploited in political action.

Propaganda, then, is conducted with symbols which are utilized as far as possible by elite and counter-elite; but the intensity of collective emotions and the broad direction and distribution of collective acts are matters of the changing total context. . . .

II / American Oratory

Oratory may be defined simply as the art of public speaking; to say what American oratory is may require some adjective like colorful or flamboyant though in recent decades it has often been maligned as old-fashioned. This is merely to say that taste and styles have changed. Later selections will prove that the art of public speaking is by no means moribund in the United States. In this section we begin with an essay by Denis Brogan on the American addiction to words, including oratory, and continue with samplings of two famous senatorial orations separated by a modern appreciation of Daniel Webster. The section ends with a delightful antidote for oratory from Finley Peter Dunne.

DENIS W. BROGAN

America Is Words

Denis W. Brogan was born in Scotland in 1900 of Irish and Scotch-Irish stock and educated at Glasgow, Oxford and Harvard Universities. Professor of political science at Cambridge University since 1943, his absorbing interest as writer and lecturer has been the political life and institutions of the United States. This selection is taken from "Unity and Liberty," a chapter in Mr. Brogan's *The American Character* which was written in 1944. It gives evidence of a warm-hearted but observant surveillance over his trans-Atlantic cousins.*

America is promises, but America is words, too. It is built like a church on a rock of dogmatic affirmations. "We hold these truths to be self-evident, that all men are created equal, that they are endowed by their Creator with certain unalienable Rights, that among these are Life, Liberty and the pursuit of Happiness." "We the People of the United States, in order to form a more perfect Union, establish Justice,

* Copyright 1944 by Denis W. Brogan. Reprinted from *The American Character* by Denis W. Brogan, Vintage Edition, by permission of Alfred A. Knopf, Inc.

insure domestic Tranquillity, provide for the common defense, promote the general Welfare, and secure the Blessings of Liberty to ourselves and our Posterity, do ordain and establish this Constitution." These are only two of the most famous assertions of faith in things unseen, of dogmatic articles denied in good faith by many non-Americans but asserted in good faith by millions of Jefferson's countrymen from July 4, 1776 to this day. How absurd an ambition for a people to attempt, by a written constitution, to "establish justice"! It is an ambition to make lawyers laugh and philosophers weep. "To promote the general welfare"; what is this entity, so confidently labeled? What would a Marxian or a Machiavellian make of it? . . .

But these aspirations, these hopes, extravagant or meaningless as they may seem to the critical, have been fighting words, hopes and beliefs leading to action. So have been the phrases, the slogans, authentic, apocryphal, half-authentic, with which American history and American memory is filled. This is no country where "what Mr. Gladstone said in 1884" is a comic mystery. These echoes from a heroic if overdramatized past resound still: "Give me liberty or give me death!" "In the name of the Great Jehovah and the Continental Congress!" "First in war, first in peace, first in the hearts of his countrymen." . . . "With malice toward none." . . . "Make the world safe for democracy." "One third of a nation." The American man-in-the-street may not attribute all these slogans correctly. . . . He may have no more knowledge of the historical context than had the badly frightened citizen who, rescued from a lynching bee, protested: "I didn't say I was against the Monroe Doctrine; I love the Monroe Doctrine, I would die for the Monroe Doctrine. I merely said I didn't know what it was." Not all his slogans are reverent. He may, at times, fall back on "Oh, yeah" or the more adequate "however you slice it, it's still baloney." But he knows too much to despise the power of speech, to think that Bryan was adequately described when he was compared to the Platte River of his native Nebraska: "Five inches deep and five miles wide at the mouth." The power of even bad oratory is still great. The power of good oratory is greater.

So the American suspends his irony when a recognized public figure is speaking, or even when he is merely "sounding off." The American audience listens patiently, even happily, to dogmatic and warm statements in favor of the American Constitution, home, woman, business, farmer. An American college president (from the deep South) has been known to impose a severe strain on the discipline of the undergraduates of an Oxford college by addressing them as "clean-limbed, clear-eyed boys." A pastor has been known to describe casting a ballot as a "political sacrament." Senator Vest's panegyric on the dog is only recently condemned as too lush, and a tribute to Southern womanhood is engraved on the pedestal of a statue to a forgotten statesman in Nashville, Tennessee.

In Chambers of Commerce, at Rotary Club meetings, at college commencements, in legislatures, in Congress, speech is treated seriously, according to the skill and taste of the user. Americans have no fear of boss words or of eloquence, no fear of clichés, no fear of bathos. In short, Americans are like all political peoples except the British. It is the countrymen of Burke and Gladstone and Asquith and Churchill who are the exception. But the difference has now the importance of an acquired characteristic. The British listener — above all, the English listener — is surprised and embarrassed by being asked to applaud statements whose truth he has no reason to doubt, but whose expression seems to him remarkably abstract and adorned with flowers of old-fashioned rhetoric. It is in Congress, not in the House of Commons, that a speaker can safely conclude a speech on the reorganization of the civil service with a parallel between the Crucifixion and what the then incumbent of the White House had to go through. It is in all kinds of American public meetings that speakers can "slate" and "rap" and "score" and "blast" — to the advantage of headline-writers. No words, it seems, can be strong enough to express the passionate feelings involved. It is not quite so bad or so good as that; American politicians, American orators, are not so burned up as they seem. But it must not be forgotten that they are often quite annoyed, quite worried, quite angry; that they are taking really quite a dim view, even when all they can find to express their mood, verbally, is an assertion that the American way of life is due to end on the first Tuesday after the first Monday in November every four years. . . .

It is not merely that Americans like slogans, like words. They like absolutes in ethics. They believe that good is good, even if they quarrel over what, in the circumstances, *is* good. It was an American, true, who said: "My country, right or wrong. May she always be right. But, right or wrong, my country."

But this sentiment is in advance of that of many simple patriots in other lands who cannot conceive that their country would be wrong, who feel no possible risk of moral strain. . . . To condemn a thing simply as un-American is often foolish, but no more foolish than to condemn a thing merely as un-English. And since the Americans are very articulate about the content of Americanism, while being English is a thing in itself, there is slightly more chance of there being meaning in "un-American" than in "un-English."

This national fondness for oratory, for slogans, has another cause or another result. It was an English Puritan leader on trial for his life who said of the execution of Charles I: "This thing was not done in a corner." It was a very American attitude. What Wilson preached — "open covenants openly arrived at" — is what the American people wants and expects to get. Like Wilson, it exaggerates the degree to which this standard of public negotiation is practicable. It is not always possible to negotiate under the klieg lights of congressional or press publicity. There are sometimes good reasons not only for secret negotiations but for confidential commitments. But they have to be very good reasons, advanced by leaders, native or foreign, in whom the American people have trust — and that trust will not be unlimited. No American leader, certainly not Washington or Lincoln, not Jackson or Jefferson at the height of their power, was thought to be above criticism or even above a certain degree of legitimate suspicion. Whitman, when he wrote of "the never-ending audacity of elected persons," voiced a general American belief that all leaders bear watching and that they are in duty bound to make frequent reports on the state of the Union, with or without aid of a fireside. The Americans are all, in this connection, from Missouri; they have got to be shown. They have also got to be told, and so has the world. Again, it is a powerful American tradition at work. Every American child used to learn by heart and many still learn by heart a famous plea for telling the world. For the most sacred of all American political scriptures, the Declaration of Independence, opens with a preamble justifying publicity. "When in the course of human events, it becomes necessary for one people to dissolve the political bonds which have connected them with another, and to assume among the Powers of the earth, the separate and equal station to which the Laws of Nature and of Nature's God entitle them, a decent respect to the opinions of mankind requires that they should declare the causes which impel them to the separation."

The Americans expect from their own leaders — and from the leaders of other countries — a regard for the "Laws of Nature and of Nature's God"; they also expect a "decent respect to the opinions of mankind" — publicly manifested in reasons given and discussed with what may seem excessive freedom and candor of comment. It is a view which gives rise to awkwardness and annoyance, but that can't be helped. The ablest modern publicist, native or foreign, is no match for one of the two greatest writers of political prose who have been Presidents of the United States. And since I have talked so much of the American passion for oratory, for the spoken word, it is worth recalling that Thomas Jefferson, one of the foremost figures in American history, was also easily the worst public speaker of his time, perhaps of any time.

"A decent respect to the opinions of mankind." It is still a phrase to be remembered. It means that the American man-in-the-street expects to get the low-down on all secret conferences, to have international decisions supplied to him before the participants have had time to put their smiles on and pose for the group photograph. If this demand is not forthcoming from official sources, it is provided from unofficial sources. Commentators of varying degrees of knowledge, candor, truthfulness, ingenuity, intelligence, explain and announce. Wildly conflicting guesses are made with equal confidence, and the reader and listener are given a wide range of confidential misinformation — as is their right. The outsider may wonder at the willing suspension of disbelief on which the commentators can count. He may think that Tom Sawyer was a notably representative American in his insistence on romantic possibilities in face of drab and dreary realities. He may wonder whether an eminent law professor has any particular authority for his views on the connection between British policy and Romanian oil. He may wonder whether anybody wanting to keep a secret would tell it to Walter Winchell or even dare to enter the Stork Club. But these doubts are irrelevant. For the dispensers of secrets are catering to a public that has a village horror of the successful privacy of its neighbors. This public could [not] see why Mr. Eisenhower should want to keep his political intentions quiet, any more than Mr. Tommy Manville keeps his matrimonial intentions quiet. Of course, he may try, as a football coach keeps his secret plays quiet if the scouts from other colleges let him. But it is the duty of columnists and senators to tell all, as soon as they have discovered it or even before. And no agreement that needs to be kept dark for any length of time has any chance of success in the United States. For the American Republic is much more like the Athenian than like the Venetian Republic. And Americans, though they have a great deal to do, have in common with Saint Paul's Athenian audience a continuous eagerness "to tell or to hear some new thing."

But there is more behind it than this passion for information, for an elaborate version of corner-grocery gossip. The American Republic was founded in the days of the *"secret du roi,"* . . . [when] great decisions were made by kings or oligarchies in secret, and the results communicated to docile subjects, this was the world against which the founders of the American Republic revolted. True, great things have been done in secret even in America. The Constitution was made in secret — it could not have been made in public even if the art of eavesdropping had in those days been practiced as expertly as it is now. But it was presented, quickly and in its final form, to the American people, presented to be accepted, or rejected, or amended. Only so could "We the People of the United States" be committed. Only so can they be committed today.

DANIEL WEBSTER

Liberty and *Union*

Daniel Webster (1782–1852) was born in New Hampshire and educated at Dartmouth College whose autonomy he was successfully to defend in a famous Supreme Court case. He first went to Congress from New Hampshire, but ambition settled him in Massachusetts and thereafter it was that state that sent him to the House and then to the Senate. This is a sampling of his second reply to Senator Hayne of South Carolina who had been expounding states' rights against the supremacy of the Union and specifically defending nullification. The four-hour oration, probably his greatest, raised Webster to the rank of the immortals and was heard thereafter wherever prizes were given for declamation. It was delivered on January 26, 1830.*

I understand the honorable gentleman from South Carolina to maintain that it is a right of the State legislatures to interfere whenever, in their judgment, this government transcends its constitutional limits, and to arrest the operation of its laws. . . .

I understand him to insist, that, if the exigency of the case, in the opinion of any State government, require it, such State government may, by its own sovereign authority, annul an act of the general government which it deems plainly and palpably unconstitutional. . . .

I say, the right of a State to annul a law of Congress cannot be maintained but on the ground of the unalienable right of man to resist oppression; that is to say, upon the ground of revolution. I admit that there is an ultimate violent remedy, above the Constitution, and in defiance of the Constitution, which may be resorted to when a revolution is to be justified. But I do not admit that under the Constitution and in conformity with it, there is any mode in which a State government, as a member of the Union, can interfere and stop the progress of the general government, by force of her own laws, under any circumstances whatever. . . .

It is observable enough, that the doctrine for which the honorable gentleman contends leads him to the necessity of maintaining, not only that this general government is the creature of the States, but that it is the creature of each of the States severally, so that each may assert the power for itself of determining whether it acts within the limits of its authority. It is the servant of four and twenty masters, of different wills and

* *Congressional Debates,* 1829–30; Vol. VI. Pt. 1, pp. 72–80 (January 26, 1830).

different purposes, and yet bound to obey all. This absurdity (for it seems no less) arises from a misconception as to the origin of this government in its true character. It is Sir, the people's Constitution, the people's government, made for the people, and answerable to the people. The people of the United States have declared that this Constitution shall be the supreme law. We must either admit the proposition, or dispute their authority. . . .

For myself, Sir, I do not admit the jurisdiction of South Carolina or any other State, to prescribe my constitutional duty; or to settle between me and the people the validity of laws of Congress for which I have voted. I decline her umpirage. . . . And, Sir, if we look to the general nature of the case, could any thing have been more preposterous than to make a government for the whole Union, and yet leave its powers subject not to one interpretation, but to thirteen, or twenty-four? . . .

And now, Mr. President, let me run the honorable gentleman's doctrine a little into its practical application. . . . We will take the existing case of the tariff law. South Carolina is said to have made up her opinion upon it . . . and will we must suppose pass a law of her legislature, declaring the several acts of Congress, usually called the tariff laws, null and void, so far as they respect South Carolina, or the citizens thereof. So far, all is a paper transaction and easy enough. But the collector at Charleston is collecting the duties imposed by these tariff laws. He, therefore, must be stopped. The collector will seize the goods if the tariff duties are not paid. The State authorities will undertake their rescue, the marshall, with his *posse,* will come to the collector's aid, and here the contest begins. The militia of the State will be called out to sustain the nullifying act. . . .

Before this military array should fall on the custom-house, collector, clerks, and all, it is very probable some of those composing it would request of their gallant commander-in-chief to be informed a little upon the point of law. . . . How, then, they would ask, do you propose to defend us? We are not afraid of bullets, but treason has a way of taking people off that we do not much relish. How do you propose to defend us? . . . "These tariff laws," he would repeat, "are unconstitutional, palpably, deliberately, dangerously." That all may be so; but if the tribunals should not happen to be of that opinion, shall we swing for it? We are ready to die for our country, but it is rather an awkward business, this dying without touching the ground! After all, that is a sort of hemp tax worse than any part of the tariff. The honorable gentleman would be in a dilemma, like that of another great general. He would have a knot before him which he could not untie. He must cut it with his sword. He must say to his followers, "Defend yourselves with your bayonets"; and this is war, — civil war. . . .

Mr. President, I have thus stated the reasons of my dissent to the doctrines which have been advanced and maintained. . . . I profess, Sir, in my career hitherto, to have kept steadily in view the prosperity and honor of the whole country, and the preservation of our Federal Union. It is to that Union that we owe our safety at home, and our consideration and dignity abroad. It is to that Union that we are chiefly indebted for whatever makes us most proud of our country. . . .

I have not allowed myself, Sir, to look beyond the Union, to see what might lie hidden in the dark recess behind. I have not coolly weighed the chances of preserving liberty when the bonds that unite us together shall be broken asunder. I have not accustomed myself to hang over the precipice of disunion, to see whether, with my short sight, I can fathom the depth of the abyss below; nor could I regard him as a safe counsellor in the affairs of this government, whose thoughts should be mainly bent on considering, not how the Union may be best preserved, but how tolerable might be the condition of the people when it shall be broken up and destroyed. While the Union lasts, we have high, exciting, gratifying prospects spread out before us, for us and our children. Beyond that I seek not to penetrate the veil. God grant that in my day, at least, that curtain may not rise! God grant that on my vision never may be opened what lies behind! When my eyes shall be turned to behold for the last time the sun in heaven, may I not see him shining on the broken and dishonored fragments of a once glorious Union; on States dissevered, discordant, belligerent; on a land rent with civil feuds, or drenched, it may be, in fraternal blood! Let their last feeble and lingering glance rather behold the gorgeous ensign of the republic, now known and honored throughout the earth, still full high advanced, its arms and trophies streaming in their original lustre, not a stripe erased or polluted, nor a single star obscured, bearing for its motto, no such miserable interrogatory as "What is all this worth?" nor those other words of delusion and folly, "Liberty first and Union afterwards"; but everywhere, spread all over in characters of living light, blazing on all its ample folds, as they float over the sea and over the land, and in every wind under the whole heavens, that other sentiment, dear to every true American heart, — Liberty *and* Union, now and forever, one and inseparable!

VAN WYCK BROOKS

Webster the Man

Van Wyck Brooks (1886–1963) was a literary critic, historian and
biographer. He was born at Plainfield, N. J., and educated at Harvard. Here he
presents a full-bodied Webster who is not only master of the spoken word but a
dynamic character of almost legendary stature.* The selection is taken from "The
New Age in Boston and Cambridge," a chapter in Brooks' The Flowering of New
England. It was written in the mid-1930's.

Of this little statesmanly world [of Boston] . . . Webster was
the great political figure. A demon of a man, a full-blooded, exuberant
Philistine, with a demiurgic brain and a bull's body, a Philistine in all
but his devotion to the welfare of the State, his deep strain of racial piety,
— this was the grand thing in Webster, — with an all-subduing personal
force, an eye as black as death and a look like a lion's, as the farmers
in his native New Hampshire said, almost a foreigner, with his rustic
manners, among these Boston lovers of elegance, he was fighting, in and
out of Congress, first for the Constitution, for the Union, imperilled by
so many factions, and secondly for the manufacturing interests that lay
behind New England's rising fortunes. With an oratorical gift as great
as Burke's — in learning, in unction, if not in cultivation, — for, while
Webster had a feeling for the sublime, he had little feeling for the beautiful, — he fought for the solid facts of property and the good old Yankee
motive of self-interest. His politics, his economic doctrines were those of
any sound New Hampshire farmer who owned a dam and a mill and
turned his dollars over to the Boston bankers. These doctrines naturally
pleased the Boston bankers. As a lawyer, he was unapproachable. When
he talked about other lawyers, he made them seem like characters in
Plutarch. He could invest a common murder-case with the atmosphere of
an Aeschylean drama.

A hunter, fisherman, farmer, who gloried in his rural avocations, in
which the traits of the backwoods pioneer were mingled with those of
an old border baron, Webster was to become, as the years went by, a
legendary figure in New England. In Boston, he was the rock of the
Constitution, as kings had been defenders of the faith. Throughout the
country districts, he was "Dan'l," whose every word, as a farmer re-

* From the book The Flowering of New England by Van Wyck Brooks. Copyright 1936,
1952, by Van Wyck Brooks. Reprinted by permission of E. P. Dutton & Co., Inc. and
J. M. Dent & Sons, Ltd.

marked, seemed to weigh a pound. People said that Dan'l was made of granite, and they knew he had learned his American history from old Captain Webster of the minute-men, who had guarded Washington's tent on the battle-field and for whom Liberty and the Union, far from being phrases, were facts that represented blood and steel. Everyone knew the great squire of Marshfield, where he had a farm as large as half a county. Everyone had heard him on the platform, every boy and girl had seen his picture, the dark brow that looked like Mount Monadnock, the wide-brimmed hat and the knee-high boots, the linsey-woolsey coat and the flowing necktie, the walking-stick that was said to be ten feet long. There was something elemental in his composition, something large and lavish. Even his faults were ample. Webster despised the traditional virtues.[1] He spent money in a grand way, borrowing and lending with equal freedom. He was far from sober, or would have been if two tumblers of brandy had been enough to put him under the table. He could be surly enough, when he had his moods of God-Almightiness, or when he wished to insult some sycophant. The thunderclouds would gather on his brow and the lightning flash from his eye, and he would tell a committee that their town was the dullest place on earth. No one could be more truculent, especially in the hay-fever season; but he was always good-natured with the farmers, who liked to think of him as their man. They knew what Webster meant when he said that his oxen were better company than the men in the Senate. They knew all his ways and the names of his guns and animals, as the Jews of old knew the weapons of Nimrod, or Abraham's flocks and herds, — his great ram Goliath, his shot-guns, "Mrs. Patrick" and "Wilmot Proviso," his trout-rod, "Old Killall." They knew he had written the Bunker Hill oration, composed it word by word with Old Killall in his hand, wading in the Marshfield River. They had heard of his tens of thousands of swine and sheep, his herds of Peruvian llamas and blooded cattle, the hundreds of thousands of trees he had raised from seed. They knew that while his guests were still asleep, — the scores of guests who were always visiting Marshfield, — he rose at four o'clock and lighted the fires, roused the cocks with his early-morning candles, milked and fed the stock and chatted in the kitchen with his farm-hands, quoting Mr. Virgil, the Roman farmer. And at Marshfield, as everyone knew, his horses were buried in a special graveyard, with all the honours of war, standing upright, with their shoes and halters.

From Boston, across New England, across the nation, Webster's fame spread, as the years advanced. Boston men who had seen Garrick and

---

[1] "Thirty years ago, when Mr. Webster at the bar or in the Senate filled the eyes and minds of young men, you might often hear cited as Mr. Webster's three rules: first, never to do today what he could defer till tomorrow; secondly, never to do himself what he could make another do for him; and, thirdly, never to pay any debt today." Emerson, *Letters and Social Aims*.

Foote and heard Burke and Sheridan, the masters of the spoken word, were satisfied that Webster was their equal. Countless thousands, bankers, lawyers, farmers, read his orations aloud by the evening fire. They felt as if the woods and the fields and the ocean had found a worthy voice in Webster's words; and Captain Thomas, his neighbor, was not the only man who longed for death when Webster met defeat. This faithful follower, fearing that all was lost, after Senator Hayne's second speech, cast away his boots, saying he would never want them more, and took to his bed for days.[2] New England had never known a public man with such a Jovian personality, whose words, when he chose to deploy them in a diplomatic encounter, had the force of a fleet of battleships. He could make the United States appear the mightiest of all historic empires. Who knew better than he, or could say it better, that America was the hope of liberty. . . . Who was more the symbol of his country? Were the Boston people, with all their self-possession, still, in a measure, tinged with colonialism? Were they prone to ask the visiting European what he thought of American institutions? Were the countryfolk too ready to protest that they had whipped the redcoats? Were the gentry still English in their customs? Webster was the universal answer. Noah Webster, with his dictionary, — whether for better or worse, — had established American usage in the matter of words. Daniel Webster was equally potent in matters of personality. All his traits, his references, his habits bore witness to the national character and buttressed it with a kind of authority that could not be gainsaid. When he spoke of the Bay State and Bunker Hill, of Plymouth Rock, Lexington and Concord, one felt that to belong to Massachusetts was the noblest privilege of history. *Civis Romanus sum.* "Thank God, I also am an American!"

[2] Webster's second reply to Hayne from which came the preceding selection must soon have restored this follower of little faith.

ALBERT J. BEVERIDGE

The Philippines Are Ours Forever

Having won oratorical prizes from adolescence on, Albert J. Beveridge (1862–1927) became United States Senator from Indiana in 1899. Before taking his seat he made himself an unimpeachable authority on empire-building by a tour of the Philippines. The treaty which brought us these islands had passed the Senate by a bare two-thirds vote, and a determined revolt of Filipino patriots appeared to strengthen the anti-imperialist case. Senator Beveridge's maiden speech of January 9, 1900, supporting a resolution to retain the Philippines, established him as the most eloquent exponent of Manifest Destiny.*

Mr. President, I address the Senate at this time because Senators and Members of the House on both sides have asked that I give to Congress and the country my observations in [sic] the Philippines and the Far East, and the conclusions which those observations compel; and because of hurtful resolutions introduced and utterances made in the Senate, every word of which will cost and is costing the lives of American soldiers.

Mr. President, the times call for candor. The Philippines are ours forever, "territory belonging to the U. S.," as the Constitution calls them. And just beyond the Philippines are China's illimitable markets. We will not retreat from either. We will not repudiate our duty in the archipelago. We will not abandon our opportunity in the Orient. We will not renounce our part in the mission of our race, trustee, under God, of the civilization of the world. And we will move forward to our work, not howling out regrets like slaves whipped to their burdens, but with gratitude for a task worthy of our strength, and thanksgiving to Almighty God that He has marked us as His chosen people, henceforth to lead in the regeneration of the world.

This island empire is the last land left in all the oceans. If it should prove a mistake to abandon it, the blunder once made would be irretrievable. If it proves a mistake to hold it, the error can be corrected when we will. Every other progressive nation stands ready to relieve us.

But to hold it will be no mistake. Our largest trade henceforth must be with Asia. The Pacific is our ocean. More and more Europe will manufacture the most it needs, secure from its colonies the most it consumes. Where shall we turn for consumers of our surplus? Geography answers the

* *Congressional Record,* Vol. 33, Pt. 1, pp. 704–712 (Washington, 1900).

question. China is our natural customer. . . . The Philippines give us a base at the door of all the East. . . .

Most future wars will be conflicts for commerce. The power that rules the Pacific, therefore, is the power that rules the world. And, with the Philippines, that power is and will forever be the American Republic. . . .

The Philippines command the commercial situation of the entire East. . . . And yet American statesmen plan to surrender this commercial throne of the Orient where Providence and our soldiers' lives have placed us. When history comes to write the story of that suggested treason to American supremacy and therefore to the spread of American civilization, let her in mercy write that those who so proposed were merely blind and nothing more. But if they did not command China, India, the Orient, the whole Pacific for purposes of offense, defence, and trade the Philippines are so valuable in themselves that we should hold them. I have cruised more than 2,000 miles through the archipelago, every moment a surprise at its loveliness and wealth. I have ridden hundreds of miles on the islands, every foot of the way a revelation of vegetable and mineral riches.

No land in America surpasses in fertility the plains and valleys of Luzon. Rice and coffee, sugar and cocoanuts, hemp and tobacco, and many products of the temperate as well as the tropic zone grow in various sections of the archipelago. . . . At Cebu the best informed man in the island told me that 40 miles of Cebu's mountain chain are practically mountains of coal. . . . I have a nugget of pure gold picked up in its present form on the banks of a Philippine creek. . . . The mineral wealth of this empire of the ocean will one day surprise the world. . . . And the wood, hemp, copra, and other products of the Philippines supply what we need and cannot ourselves produce. . . . If we are willing to go to war rather than let England have a few feet of frozen Alaska, which affords no market and commands none, what should we not do rather than let England, Germany, Russia or Japan have all the Philippines? And no man on the spot can fail to see that this would be their fate if we retired. . . .

Here then Senators is the situation. Two years ago there was no land in all the world which we could occupy for any purpose. Our commerce was daily turning toward the Orient, and geography and trade developments made necessary our commercial empire over the Pacific. And in that ocean we had no commercial, naval, or military base. Today we have one of the three great ocean possessions of the globe, located at the most commanding commercial, naval and military points in the eastern seas, within hail of India, shoulder to shoulder with China, richer in its own resources than any equal body of land on the entire globe, and peopled by a race which civilization demands shall be improved. Shall we abandon it? That man little knows the common people of the Republic, little understands the instincts of our race, who thinks we will not hold it fast and hold it forever. . . .

But Senators it would be better to abandon this combined garden and Gibraltar of the Pacific, and count our blood and treasure already spent a profitable loss, than to apply any academic arrangement of self-government to these children. They are not capable of self-government. How could they be? They are not of a self-governing race. They are Orientals, Malays, instructed by Spaniards in the latter's worst estate. They know nothing of practical government except as they have witnessed the weak, corrupt, cruel and capricious rule of Spain. . . .

No one need fear their competition with our labor. No reward beguile, no force compel, these children of indolence to leave their trifling lives for the fierce and fervid industry of high-wrought America. The very reverse is the fact. . . .

Mr. President, self-government and internal development have been the dominant notes of our first century; administration and development of other lands will be the dominant notes of our second century. . . . Administration of good government is not denial of liberty. For what is liberty? It is not savagery. . . . The Declaration of Independence does not forbid us to do our part in the regeneration of the world. If it did, the Declaration would be wrong. . . . The Declaration applies only to people capable of self-government. How dare any man prostitute this expression of the very elect of self-governing people to a race of Malay children of barbarism, schooled in Spanish methods and ideas?

Mr. President, this question is deeper than any question of party politics; deeper than any question of the isolated policy of our country even; deeper even than any question of constitutional power. It is elemental. It is racial. God had not been preparing the English-speaking and Teutonic peoples for a thousand years for nothing but vain and idle self-contemplation and self-admiration. No! He has made us the master organizers of the world to establish system where chaos reigns. He has given us the spirit of progress to overwhelm the forces of reaction throughout the earth. He has made us adepts in government that we may administer government among savage and senile peoples. Were it not for such a force as this the world would relapse into barbarism and night. And of all our race He has marked the American people as His chosen nation to finally lead in the regeneration of the world. This is the divine mission of America, and it holds for us all the profit, all the glory, all the happiness possible to man. We are trustees of the world's progress, guardians of its righteous peace. . . .

What shall history say of us? Shall it say that we renounced that holy trust, left the savage to his base condition, the wilderness to the reign of waste, deserted duty, abandoned glory, forgot our sordid profit even, because we feared our strength and read the charter of our power with the doubter's eye and the quibbler's mind? Shall it say that, called by events to captain and command the proudest, ablest, purest race of history in history's noblest work, we declined that commission? Our fathers would not have had it so. No! They founded no paralytic government, incapable of the simplest acts of administration. They planted no sluggard people, passive while the world's work calls them. They established no reactionary nation. They unfurled no retreating flag.

That flag has never paused in its onward march. Who dares halt it now — now, when history's largest events are carrying it forward; now, when we are at last one people, strong enough for any task, great enough for any glory destiny can bestow? How comes it that our first century closes with the process of consolidating the American people into a unit just accomplished, and quick upon the stroke of that great hour presses upon us our world opportunity, world duty, and world glory, which none but a people welded into an indivisible nation can achieve or perform? Blind indeed is he who sees not the hand of God in events so vast, so harmonious, so benign. Reactionary indeed is the mind that perceives not that this vital people is the strongest of the saving forces of the world; that our place, therefore, is at the head of the constructing and redeeming nations of the earth; and that to stand aside while events march on is a surrender of our interests, a betrayal of our duty as blind as it is base. Craven indeed is the heart that fears to perform a work so golden and so noble; that dares not win a glory so immortal. . . .

And so, Senators, with reverent hearts, where dwells the fear of God, the American people move forward to the future of their hope and the doing of His work.

Mr. President and Senators, adopt the resolution offered, that peace may come quickly and that we may begin our saving, regenerating and uplifting work. Adopt it and this bloodshed will cease when these deluded children of our islands learn that this is the final word of the representatives of the American people in Congress assembled. Reject it, and the world, history and the American people will know where to forever fix the awful responsibility for the consequences that will surely follow such failure to do our manifest duty. How dare we delay when our soldiers' blood is flowing?

FINLEY PETER DUNNE

Mr. Dooley on Taking the Philippines

This is a searching comment on Senator Beveridge's philosophy of empire-building, though it preceded the speech. Finley Peter Dunne (1867–1936) was an American satirist whose columns in Chicago newspapers left political pretension and bombast no hiding place. In this piece Mack is of course President McKinley, and George is Admiral Dewey, who sank the Spanish fleet in Manila Bay. Mr. Dooley is the tirelessly questioning, skeptical bartender.* The time was late in 1898.

"I know what I'd do if I was Mack," said Mr. Hennessy. "I'd hist a flag over the Ph'lippeens, an' I'd take in th' whole lot iv thim."

"An' yet," said Mr. Dooley, "tis not more thin two months since ye larned whether they were islands or canned goods. . . . Suppose ye was standin' at th' corner iv State Sthreet an' Archey R-road, wud ye know what car to take to get to th' Ph'lippeens? If yer son Packy was to ask ye where th' Ph-lippeens is, cud ye give him anny good idea whether they was in Rooshia or jus' west iv th' thracks?"

"Mebbe I cudden't," said Mr. Hennessy, haughtily, "but I'm f'r takin' them in, annyhow."

"So might I be," said Mr. Dooley, "if I cud on'y get me mind on it. Wan iv the worst things about this here war is th' way it's makin' puzzles f'r our poor, tired heads. Whin I wint into it, I thought all I'd have to do was to set up here behind th' bar with a good tin-cint see-gar in me teeth, an' toss dinnymite bombs into th' hated city iv Havana. But look at me now. Th' war is still goin' on; an' ivry night, whin I'm countin' up the cash, I'm askin' mesilf will I annex Cubia or lave it to the Cubians? Will I take Porther Ricky or put it by? An' what shud I do with the Ph'lippeens? Oh, what shud I do with thim? I can't annex thim because I don't know where they ar-re. I can't let go iv thim because some wan else'll take thim if I do. They are eight thousan' iv thim islands, with a popylation iv wan hundherd millyon naked savages; an' me bedroom's crowded now with me an' th' bed. How can I take thim in, an' how on earth am I goin' to cover th' nakedness iv thim savages with me wan shoot iv clothes? An' yet 'twud break me heart to think iv givin' people I niver see or heerd tell iv back to other people I don't know. An', if I don't take thim, Schwartzmeister down th' sthreet, that has half me thrade already, will grab thim sure.

* From Finley Peter Dunne, *Mr. Dooley in Peace and in War* (Boston, 1899) pp. 43–48.

"It ain't that I'm afraid iv not doin' th' r-right thing in th' end, Hinnissy. Some mornin' I'll wake up an' know jus' what to do, an' that I'll do. But 'tis th' annoyance in th' mane time. I've been r-readin' about th' counthry. 'Tis over beyant ye'er left shoulder whin ye're facin' east. Jus' throw ye'er thumb back, an' ye have it as ac'rate as anny man in town. 'Tis farther thin Boohlgahrya an' not so far as Blewchoochoo. It's near Chiny, an' it's not so near; an', if a man was to bore a well through fr'm Goshen, Indianny, he might sthrike it, an' thin again he might not. It's a poverty-sthricken counthry, full iv goold an' precious stones, where th' people can pick dinner off th' threes an' ar-re starvin' because they have no stepladders. Th' inhabitants is mostly naygurs an' Chinnymen, peaceful, industhrus, an' law-abidin', but savage an' bloodthirsty in their methods. They wear no clothes except what they have on, an' each woman has five husbands an' each man has five wives. Th' r-rest goes into th' discard, th' same as here. Th' islands has been ownded be Spain since befure th' fire; an' she's threated thim so well they're now up in ar-rms again her, except a majority iv thim which is thurly loyal. Th' natives seldom fight, but whin they get mad at wan another they r-run-a-muck. Whin a man r-runs-a-muck, sometimes they hang him an' sometimes they discharge him an' hire a new motorman. Th' women ar-re beautiful, with languishin' black eyes, an' they smoke see-gars, but ar-re hurried an' incomplete in their dhress. I see a pitcher iv wan th' other day with nawthin' on her but a basket of cocoanuts an' a hoop-skirt. They're no prudes. We import juke, hemp, cigar wrappers, sugar, an' fairy tales fr'm th' Ph'lippeens, an' export six-inch shells an' the like. Iv late th' Ph'lippeens has awaked to th' fact that they're behind th' times, an' has received much American amminition in their midst. They say th' Spanyards is all tore up about it.

"I larned all this fr'm th' papers, an' I know 'tis sthraight. An' yet, Hinnissy, I dinnaw what to do about th' Ph'lippeens. An' I'm all alone in th' wurruld. Ivrybody else has made up his mind. Ye ask anny conducthor on Ar-rchy R-road, an' he'll tell ye. Ye can find out fr'm the papers; an', if ye really want to know, all ye have to do is to ask a promnent citizen who can mow all th' lawn he owns with a safety razor. But I don't know."

"Hang on to thim," said Mr. Hennessy, stoutly. "What we've got we must hold."

"Well," said Mr. Dooley, "if I was Mack, I'd lave it to George. I'd say: 'George,' I'd say, 'if ye're f'r hangin' on, hang on it is. If ye say, lave go, I dhrop thim.'" Twas George won thim with th' shells, an' th' question's up to him."

III
The Rhetoric of Freedom

Freedom is of many kinds and its rhetoric has never been standardized. Our first selection is taken from Adam Smith's *Wealth of Nations* which made the classic case for economic freedom. This is followed by R. H. Tawney who is concerned with the human cost of economic freedom, and by de Tocqueville who doubts that there can be much freedom where the majority rules. The final selection is a speech by Judge Learned Hand whose interest in freedom goes beyond the political and economic.

ADAM SMITH

Free Trade Is Nature's Way

Adam Smith (1723–1790) was born in Scotland, educated at Oxford and finally settled into the chair of moral philosophy at the University of Glasgow. His advocacy of *laissez faire* brought him great acclaim in the 19th century as Britain put his precepts into effect. Here in the year of the Declaration of Independence he reveals his low opinion of the politician, and his key conviction that individual self-interest is the best guide to social welfare. This is taken from a section of *The Wealth of Nations* that deals with "Restraints upon the Importation of Goods." *

By restraining, either by high duties or by absolute prohibitions, the importation of such goods from foreign countries as can be produced at home, the monopoly of the home market is more or less secured to the domestic industry employed in producing them . . .

That this monopoly of the home market frequently gives great encouragement to that particular species of industry which enjoys it, and frequently turns towards that employment a greater share of both the

* From Adam Smith, *An Inquiry into the Nature and Causes of the Wealth of Nations* (Edinburgh, 1828) Vol. II, pp. 274–307.

labor and stock of the society than would otherwise have gone to it, cannot be doubted. But whether it tends either to increase the general industry of the society, or to give it the most advantageous direction, is not, perhaps, altogether so evident. . . .

No regulation of commerce can increase the quantity of industry in any society beyond what its capital can maintain. It can only divert a part of it into a direction into which it might not otherwise have gone; and it is by no means certain that this artificial direction is likely to be more advantageous to the society than that into which it would have gone of its own accord.

Every individual is continually exerting himself to find out the most advantageous employment for whatever capital he can command. It is his own advantage, indeed, and not that of the society, which he has in view. But the study of his own advantage naturally, or rather necessarily, leads him to prefer that employment which is most advantageous to the society . . .

By preferring the support of domestic to that of foreign industry . . . he intends only his own gain, and he is in this, as in many other cases, led by an invisible hand to promote an end which was no part of his intention. Nor is it always the worse for the society that it was no part of it. By pursuing his own interest he frequently promotes that of the society more effectually than when he really intends to promote it. I have never known much good done by those who affected to trade for the public good. . . .

What is the species of domestic industry which his capital can employ, and of which the produce is likely to be of the greatest value, every individual, it is evident, can, in his local situation, judge much better than any statesman or lawgiver can do for him. The statesman who should attempt to direct private people in what manner they ought to employ their capitals would not only load himself with a most unnecessary attention, but assume an authority which could safely be trusted, not only to no single person, but to no council or senate whatever, and which would nowhere be so dangerous as in the hands of a man who had folly and presumption enough to fancy himself fit to exercise it.

To give the monopoly of the home market to the produce of domestic industry, in any particular art or manufacture, is in some measure to direct private people in what manner they ought to employ their capitals, and must, in almost all cases, be either a useless or a hurtful regulation. If the produce of domestic can be brought there [to the home market] as cheap as that of foreign industry, the regulation is evidently useless. If it cannot, it must generally be hurtful. It is the maxim of every prudent master of a family never to attempt to make at home what it will cost him more to make than to buy. The tailor does not attempt to make his own shoes, but buys them of the shoemaker. The shoemaker does not attempt to make his own clothes, but employs a tailor. The farmer attempts to make neither the one nor the other, but employs those different artificers. . . .

What is prudence in the conduct of every private family can scarce be folly in that of a great kingdom. If a foreign country can supply us with a commodity cheaper than we ourselves can make it, better buy it of them with some part of the produce of our own industry, employed in a way in which we have some advantage. . . .

The natural advantages which one country has over another in producing particular commodities are sometimes so great that it is acknowledged by all the world to be in vain to struggle with them. By means of glasses, hotbeds, and hot walls, very good grapes can be raised in Scotland, and very good wine too can be made of them at about thirty times the expense for which at least equally good can be brought from foreign countries. Would it be a reasonable law to prohibit the importation of all foreign wines merely to encourage the making of claret and burgundy in Scotland? But if there would be a manifest absurdity in turning towards any employment thirty times more of the capital and industry of the country than would be necessary to purchase from foreign countries an equal quantity of the commodities wanted, there must be an absurdity, though not altogether so glaring, yet exactly of the same kind, in turning towards any such employment a thirtieth, or even a three-hundredth part more of either. . . .

There seem, however, to be two cases in which it will generally be advantageous to lay some burden upon foreign for the encouragement of domestic industry. The first is, when some particular sort of industry is necessary for the defence of the country. The defence of Great Britain, for example, depends very much upon the number of its sailors and shipping. The act of navigation, therefore, very properly endeavors to give the sailors and shipping of Great Britain the monopoly of the trade of their own country. . . . The second case, in which it will generally be advantageous to lay some burden upon foreign for the encouragement of domestic industry is, when some tax is imposed at home upon the produce of the latter. . . .

[Also] it may sometimes be a matter of deliberation how far it is proper to continue the free importation of certain foreign goods . . . when some foreign nation restrains by high duties or prohibitions the importation of some of our manufactures into their country. Revenge in this case naturally dictates retaliation. . . . There may be good policy in retaliations of this kind, when there is a probability that they will procure the repeal of the high duties or prohibitions complained of. The recovery of a great foreign market will generally more than compensate the transitory inconveniency of paying dearer during a short time for some sorts of goods. To judge whether such retaliations are likely to produce such an effect does not, perhaps, belong so much to the science of a legislator, whose deliberations ought to be governed by general principles which are always the same, as to the skill of that insidious and crafty animal, vulgarly called a statesman or politician, whose councils are directed by the momentary fluctuations of affairs. When there is no probability that any such repeal can be procured, it seems a bad method of compensating the injury done to certain classes of our people to do another injury ourselves, not only to those classes, but to almost all the other classes of them. . . .

To expect that the freedom of trade should ever be entirely restored in Great Britain is as absurd as to expect that an Oceana or Utopia should ever be established in it. Not only the prejudices of the public, but what is much more unconquerable, the private interests of many individuals, irresistibly oppose it. Were the officers of the army to oppose with the same zeal and unanimity any reduction in the number of forces with which master manufacturers set themselves against every law that is likely to increase the number of their rivals in the home market; were the former to animate their soldiers in the same manner as the latter inflame their workmen to attack with violence and outrage the proposers of any such regulation, to attempt to reduce the army would be as dangerous as it has now become to attempt to diminish in any respect the monopoly which our manufacturers have obtained against us. This monopoly has so much increased the number of some particular tribes of them that, like an overgrown standing army, they have become formidable to the government, and upon many occasions intimidate the legislature. The member of parliament who supports every proposal for strengthening this monopoly is sure to acquire not only the reputation of understanding trade, but great popularity and influence with an order of men whose numbers and wealth render them of great importance. If he opposes them, on the contrary, and still more if he has authority enough to be able to thwart them, neither the most acknowledged probity, nor the highest rank, nor the greatest public services can protect him from the most infamous abuse and detraction, from personal insults, nor sometimes from real danger, arising from the insolent outrage of furious and disappointed monopolists.

The undertaker of a great manufacture, who, by the home markets being suddenly laid open to the competition of foreigners, should be obliged to abandon his trade, would no doubt suffer very considerably. . . . The equitable regard, therefore, to his interest requires that changes of this kind should never be introduced suddenly, but slowly, gradually, and after a very long warning. The legislature, were it possible that its deliberations could be always directed, not by the clamorous importunity of partial interests, but by an extensive view of the general good, ought upon this very account, perhaps, to be particularly careful neither to establish any new monopolies of this kind, nor to extend further those which are already established. Every such regulation introduces some degree of real disorder into the constitution of the state, which it will be difficult afterwards to cure without occasioning another disorder. . . .

R. H. TAWNEY

Freedom and Economic Inequality

The English scholar, R. H. Tawney (1880–1962), was educated at Rugby and Oxford, taught at the University of London. A life-long student of the British economy, Professor Tawney was no friend of *laissez faire*, and much of his writing was designed to undermine the institutions Adam Smith had so persuasively buttressed. This essay is taken from a chapter on "The Conditions of Economic Freedom" in his book, *Equality*, which was published in 1931.*

Freedom is always, no doubt, a matter of degree; no man enjoys all the requirements of full personal development, and all men possess some of them. It is not only compatible with conditions in which all men are fellow-servants, but would find in such conditions its most perfect expression. What it excludes is a society where only some are servants, while others are masters.

For, whatever else the idea involves, it implies, at least, that no man shall be amenable to an authority which is arbitrary in its proceedings, exhorbitant in its demands, or incapable of being called to account when it abuses its office for personal advantage. In so far as his livelihood is at the mercy of an irresponsible superior, whether political or economic, who can compel his reluctant obedience by *force majeure,* whose actions he is unable to modify or resist, save at the cost of grave personal injury to himself and his dependents, and whose favor he must court, even when he despises it, he may possess a profusion of more tangible blessings, from beer to motor-bicycles, but he can hardly be said to be in possession of freedom. . . .

Political principles resemble military tactics; they are usually designed for a war which is over. Freedom is commonly interpreted in political terms, because it was in the political arena that the most resounding of its

* From R. H. Tawney, *Equality* (London, 1931) pp. 242–255. Reprinted by permission of George Allen & Unwin, Ltd.

recent victories were won. It is regarded as belonging to human beings as citizens, rather than to citizens as human beings; so that it is possible for a nation, the majority of whose members have as little influence on the decisions that determine their economic destinies as on the motions of the planets, to applaud the idea with self-congratulatory gestures of decorous enthusiasm, as though history were of the past, but not of the present. If the attitude of the ages from which it inherits a belief in liberty had been equally ladylike, there would have been, it is probable, little liberty to applaud. . . .

The extension of liberty from the political sphere . . . [to the sphere] of economic relations is evidently among the most urgent tasks of industrial communities . . . It is evident also, however, that, in so far as this extension takes place, the traditional antithesis between liberty and equality will no longer be valid. As long as liberty is interpreted as consisting exclusively in security against oppression by the agents of the State, or as a share in its government, it is plausible, perhaps, to dissociate it from equality; for, though experience suggests that, even in this meagre and restricted sense, it is not easily maintained in the presence of extreme disparities of wealth and influence, it is possible for it to be enjoyed, in form at least, by pauper and millionaire. Such disparities, however, though they do not enable one group to become the political master of another necessarily cause it to exercise a preponderant, and sometimes an overwhelming, influence on the economic life of the rest of the community.

Hence, when liberty is construed realistically, as implying, not merely a minimum of civil and political rights, but securities that the economically weak will not be at the mercy of the economically strong, and that the control of those aspects of economic life by which all are affected will be amenable, in the last resort, to the will of all, a large measure of equality, so far from being inimical to liberty, is essential to it. In conditions which impose cooperative, rather than merely individual, effort, liberty is, in fact, equality in action, in the sense, not that all men perform identical functions or wield the same degree of power, but that all men are equally protected against the abuse of power, and equally entitled to insist that power shall be used, not for personal ends, but for the general advantage. Civil and political liberty obviously imply, not that all men shall be members of parliament, cabinet ministers, or civil servants, but the absence of such civil and political inequalities as enable one class to impose its will on another by legal coercion. It should be not less obvious that economic liberty implies, not that all men shall initiate, plan, direct, manage or administer, but the absence of such economic inequalities as can be used as a means of economic restraint.

The danger to liberty which is caused by inequality varies with differences of economic organization and public policy. . . . Among the numerous interesting phenomena which impress the foreign observer of American economic life, not the least interesting, perhaps, is the occasional emergence of industrial enterprises which appear to them, and indeed to some Americans, to have developed the characteristics, not merely of an economic undertaking, but of a kind of polity. . . . Some of them own, not merely the plant and equipment of industry, but the homes of the workers, the streets through which they pass to work, and the halls in which, if they are allowed to meet, their meetings must be held; they employ private spies and detectives, private police and, sometimes, it appears, private troops, and engage, when they deem it expedient, in private war; while organized themselves, they forbid organization among their employees, and enforce their will by evicting malcontents from their homes, and even, on occasion, by the use of armed force. . . .

The conventional assertion that inequality is inseparable from liberty is obviously, in such circumstances, unreal and unconvincing; for the existence of the former is a menace to the latter, and the latter is most likely to be secured by curtailing the former. It is true, of course, that inequalities of economic power, with the consequences they entail, are a matter of degree. It is true that in Europe, where the most portentous of the species have gone the way of the dinosaur and the ichthyosaurus, the behavior of their descendents, relying, as they must, more on brains and less on force, is respectable and sedate. In England, at any rate, where three generations of trade unionism and state intervention have partially domesticated it, the creature, to do it justice, does not roar intolerably. It is cramped by agreements on this side and legislation on that, while periodically it submits, with soft gnashings of teeth, to a major operation, which insinuates germs of sociability into its primeval roughness. Hence, it is rarely ferocious today, unless it is alarmed, and its paroxysms, when they occur, are of moderate duration.

Even in England, however . . . it can hardly be argued that the routine of economic life is so entirely unaffected by inequalities of economic power between property-owners and wage-earners that the general liberty has nothing to fear from them . . . The truth is that, when the economic scales are so unevenly weighted, to interpret liberty as a political principle, which belongs to one world, the world of politics and government, while equality belongs — if, indeed, it belongs anywhere — to another world, the world of economic affairs, is to do violence to realities. Governments, it is true, exercise powers of a great and special kind, and freedom requires that they should be held strictly to account. But the administration of things is not easily distinguished, under modern conditions of mass organization, from the control of persons, and both are in the hands, to some not inconsiderable degree, of the minority who move the levers of the economic mechanism. The truth of the matter is put by Professor Pollard in his admirable study, *The Evolution of Parliament.*

There is only one solution (he writes) of the problem of liberty, and it lies in equality. . . . Men vary in physical strength; but so far as their social relations go that inequality has been abolished. . . . Yet there must have been a period in social evolution when this refusal to permit the strong man to do what he liked with his own physical strength seemed, at least to the strong, an outrageous interference with personal liberty. . . . There is, in fact, no more reason why a man should be allowed to use his wealth or his brain than his physical strength as he likes. . . . The liberty of the weak depends upon the restraint of the strong, that of the poor upon the restraint of the rich, and that of the simpler-minded upon the restraint of the sharper. Every man should have this liberty and no more, to do unto others as he would that they should do unto him; upon that common foundation rest liberty, equality and morality. . . .

ALEXIS DE TOCQUEVILLE

Tyranny of the Majority

Following his tour of America in 1830–31, Alexis de Tocqueville (1805–59) returned to France and wrote his classic *Democracy in America.* We were flattered, and generally delighted; but insisted that the French nobleman was dead wrong about the tyranny of the majority. However in 1938, Yale's distinguished de Tocqueville scholar, George W. Pierson, suggested that the Frenchman's "grievous error" might yet be cited as further proof of his "uncanny perspicacity." *

The very essence of democratic government consists in the absolute sovereignty of the majority; for there is nothing in democratic states that is capable of resisting it. Most of the American constitutions have sought to increase this natural strength of the majority by artificial means. . . . Custom has done even more than law. It frequently happens that the voters, on electing a delegate, point out a certain line of conduct to him, and impose upon him certain positive obligations which he is pledged to fulfill. With the exception of the tumult, this comes to the same thing as if the majority itself held its deliberations in the marketplace.

Several other circumstances concur to render the power of the majority in America not only preponderant, but irresistible. The moral authority

* From Alexis de Tocqueville, *Democracy in America*, trans. by Henry Reeve (Cambridge, 1862) pp. 324–42.

of the majority is partly based upon the notion that there is more intelligence and wisdom in a number of men united than in a single individual, and that the number of the legislators is more important than their quality. The theory of equality is thus applied to the intellects of men . . .

The moral power of the majority is founded upon yet another principle, which is that the interests of the many are to be preferred to those of the few. . . .

If there existed in America a class of citizens whom the legislating majority sought to deprive of exclusive privileges which they had possessed for ages, and to bring down from an elevated station to the level of the multitude, it is probable that the minority would be less ready to submit to its laws. But as the United States were colonized by men holding equal rank, there is as yet no natural or permanent disagreement between the interests of its different inhabitants. . . .

In the United States . . . all parties are willing to recognize the rights of the majority, because they all hope at some time to be able to exercise them to their own advantage. The majority, therefore, in that country exercise a prodigious actual authority, and a power of opinion which is nearly as great; no obstacles exist which can impede or even retard its progress, so as to make it heed the complaints of those whom it crushes upon its path. This state of things is harmful in itself, and dangerous for the future. . . .

I hold it to be an impious and detestable maxim that, politically speaking, the people have a right to do anything; and yet I have asserted that all authority originates in the will of the majority. Am I, then, in contradiction with myself? . . .

When I refuse to obey an unjust law, I do not contest the right of the majority to command, but I simply appeal from the sovereignty of the people to the sovereignty of mankind. Some have not feared to assert that a people can never outstep the boundaries of justice and reason in those affairs which are peculiarly its own; and that consequently full power may be given to the majority by which they are represented. But this is the language of a slave. . . .

Unlimited power is in itself a bad and dangerous thing. Human beings are not competent to exercise it with discretion. God alone can be omnipotent, because his wisdom and his justice are always equal to his power. There is no power on earth so worthy of honor in itself or clothed with rights so sacred that I would admit its uncontrolled and all-predominant authority. When I see that the right and the means of absolute command are conferred on any power whatever, be it called a people or a king, an aristocracy or a democracy, a monarchy or a republic, I say there is the germ of tyranny, and I seek to live elsewhere, under other laws.

In my opinion, the main evil of the present democratic institutions of the United States does not arise, as is often asserted in Europe, from their weakness, but from their irresistible strength. I am not so much alarmed at the excessive liberty which reigns in that country as at the inadequate securities which one finds there against tyranny.

When an individual or a party is wronged in the United States, to whom can he apply for redress? If to public opinion, public opinion constitutes the majority; if to the legislature, it represents the majority and implicitly obeys it; if to the executive power, it is appointed by the majority and serves as a passive tool in its hands. The public force consists of the majority under arms; the jury is the majority invested with the right of hearing judicial cases; and in certain states even the judges are elected by the majority. However iniquitous or absurd the measure of which you complain, you must submit to it as well as you can. . . .

I do not say that there is a frequent use of tyranny in America at the present day; but I maintain that there is no sure barrier against it, and that the causes which mitigate the government there are to be found in the circumstances and the manners of the country more than in its laws. . . .

It is in the examination of the exercise of thought in the United States that we clearly perceive how far the power of the majority surpasses all the powers with which we are acquainted in Europe. Thought is an invisible and subtile power that mocks all the efforts of tyranny. At the present time the most absolute monarchs in Europe cannot prevent certain opinions hostile to their authority from circulating in secret through their dominions and even in their courts. It is not so in America; as long as the majority is still undecided, discussion is carried on; but as soon as its decision is irrevocably pronounced, everyone is silent, and the friends as well as the opponents of the measure unite in assenting to its propriety. The reason for this is perfectly clear: no monarch is so absolute as to combine all the powers of society in his own hands and to conquer all opposition, as a majority is able to do, which has the right both of making and of executing the laws. . . .

I know of no country in which there is so little independence of mind and real freedom of discussion as in America. In any constitutional state in Europe every sort of religious and political theory may be freely preached and disseminated; for there is no country in Europe so subdued by any single authority as not to protect the man who raises his voice in the cause of truth from the consequences of his hardihood. If he is unfortunate enough to live under an absolute government, the people are often upon his side; if he inhabits a free country, he can, if necessary, find a shelter behind the throne. The aristocratic part of society supports him in some countries, and the democracy in others. But in a nation where democratic institutions exist, organized like those of the United States, there is but one authority, one element of strength and success, with nothing beyond it.

In America the majority raises formidable barriers around the liberty of opinion; within these barriers an author may write what he pleases, but woe to him if he goes beyond them. Not that he is in danger of an *auto-da-fé*, but he is exposed to continued obloquy and persecution. His political career is closed forever, since he has offended the only authority that is able to open it. Every sort of compensation, even that of celebrity, is refused to him. Before making public his opinions he thought he had sympathizers; now it seems to him that he has none any more since he has revealed himself to everyone; then those who blame him criticize loudly and those who think as he does keep quiet and move away without courage. He yields at length, overcome by the daily effort which he has to make, and subsides into silence, as if he felt remorse for having spoken the truth. . . .

Works have been published in the proudest nations of the Old World expressly intended to censure the vices and the follies of the times: Labruyère inhabited the palace of Louis XIV when he composed his chapter upon the Great, and Moliere criticized the courtiers in the pieces that were acted before the court. But the ruling power in the United States is not to be made game of. The smallest reproach irritates its sensibility, and the slightest joke which has any foundation in truth renders it indignant; from the forms of its language up to the solid virtues of its character, everything must be made the subject of encomium. No writer, whatever be his eminence, can escape paying this tribute of adulation to his fellow citizens. The majority lives in the perpetual utterance of self-applause, and there are certain truths which the Americans can only learn from strangers or from experience. . . .

The tendencies that I have just mentioned are as yet but slightly perceptible in political society, but they already exercise an unfavorable influence upon the national character of the Americans. I attribute the small number of distinguished men in political life to the ever increasing despotism of the majority in the United States. . . .

In that immense crowd which throngs the avenues to power in the United States, I found very few men who displayed that manly candor and masculine independence of opinion which frequently distinguished the Americans in former times, and which constitutes the leading feature in distinguished characters wherever they may be found. It seems at first sight as if all the minds of the Americans were formed upon one model, so accurately do they follow the same route. A stranger does, indeed, sometimes meet with Americans who dissent from the rigor of these formularies, — with men who deplore the defects of the laws, the mutability and the ignorance of democracy, who even go so far as to observe the evil tendencies which impair the national character, and to point out such remedies as it might be possible to apply; but no one is there to hear them except yourself, and you, to whom these secret reflections are confided, are a stranger and a bird of passage. They are very ready to communicate truths which are useless to you, but they hold a different language in public.

If these lines are ever read in America, I am well assured of two things: in the first place, that all who peruse them will raise their voices to condemn me; and, in the second place, that many of them will acquit me at the bottom of their conscience.

JUDGE LEARNED HAND

The Meaning of Liberty

Judge Learned Hand was born in Albany, N. Y., in 1872, educated at Harvard College where he majored in philosophy, and at Harvard Law School, practised law in New York City, and was Judge of the United States Circuit Court, 2nd Circuit, from 1924 to his retirement in 1951. Known for his wisdom and humanity, Judge Hand gave this address on liberty on May 10, 1941, when Hitler had darkened most of Europe and no one could see how the night would end.* Judge Hand died in 1961.

I have chosen for the subject of my talk, "Liberty." When I say that I chose it, I am not speaking quite the truth; rather it chose itself. I was so acutely aware of the quicksands and wastes which await the explorer in that region that I tried to avoid an expedition into it. Perhaps a judge is especially aware of these; his colleagues are constantly assuring him that all he needs is to avoid license and anarchy on the one hand, and tyranny and despotism on the other; if he will only stick to that simple admonition he is sure to arrive. That is not very encouraging as a starter; but what gives the task its real difficulty is that the word is so charged with passion. About none is written a more fiery record of suffering and heroism; it is the center and the kernel of that inner life for which men will fight and die who will fight and die for anything. Furthermore, and perhaps for that reason it has been the rallying cry of those who hold quite opposite beliefs; one can say of it after Lincoln: "Both sides pray to it and each invokes its aid against the other." Few stop to ask what they mean, and those who do soon find the answer

---

* Address delivered before the Elizabethan Club of Yale, May 10, 1941. Printed at the Overbrook Press. Reprinted by the kind permission of the Yale Alumni Magazine.

baffling and uncertain. Why then should I venture to talk about it here tonight? Only because I could not help it. In such a world as this, so wretched and so riven, where men and women are suffering misery, mutilation, and death in the name of Liberty — whatever it may be — how can anyone be content who does not try to come to at least a tentative conclusion with himself about it? . . .

I do not know how it is with you, but my own first spontaneous response to the word is negative; I think that I am free when I can do what I want; this tiny protoplasmal center of radiant energy demands that alien impacts shall not thwart its insistences and its self-assertions. What are these? We can start with a dictum attributed to Lawrence Henderson that they consist in the performance of our accustomed rituals. . . . Each has a vested right in his freedom grounded in the deepest of foundations, the current liturgies of the society to which he belongs. Since, so conceived, Liberty is negative, one freedom is as good as another; there is no objective standard except for blind partisans of the *status quo,* whatever it may be. The rite of burying the aged alive, whatever the aged may say against it, has equal sanction with that of providing a college education for those who are not fit to receive one.

Let us then look for an objective standard. Surely we can safely begin with the satisfaction of our primitive needs. We must eat, sleep, be clothed and sheltered, and have our mates and our children. It is irrelevant that the Universe so often denies us these; we are considering hindrances by our fellows. Shall we say then that, so far as they deny us such goods, they deny our Liberty?

"Do not waste our time in trivialities," you will answer, "we must of course yield these in part, and other desires scarcely less imperious; but by doing so we create civilized society so that our life shall not be 'short, brutish, and nasty.'" . . .

No doubt; but if we press the inquiry a little further, it gets more real. . . . If we declare that a freeman will yield so far, but only so far as, having with entire detachment weighed his own good against his neighbor's, he finds the neighbor's better, that does not tell us how he is to decide which of the two is in fact the better. Of course there is the initial obstacle that entire detachment is an obvious fiction. To proceed at all we must set up some persons in our society with authority — like Plato's Guardians for instance — to whom we can depute the weighing of one good against another. . . .

Let me start with an example drawn from Plato's own city; not because we need doubt the answer, but because it illustrates the incommensurability of the elements that must be measured. When at times I hear, as we all do, some cultivated snob vaporing about the perfection of life in Athens, say from 480 to 430 B.C., and how it was the apex of civilization, someone is sure to interject that it was not so at all; rather that Athens was a hideous nightmare; that these supposed specimens of ultimate human perfection were shameless exploiters of a far greater number of other men whose misery, when matched against their own splendors, makes Stygian blackness to the eyes of all just and humane persons. . . . Supposing that an ethical or hedonistic calculus were possible, and supposing that there were no other means than the exploitation of the exploited by which the lives of the Athenian citizens could have been what they were, and supposing that these were as perfect as both he and the cultivated snob seemed to agree they were; how could he guess which way the beam would tip if one put the lives of the citizens in one scale and the good things of which they deprived the slaves in the other. . . .

At any rate I know that, whatever he said, he could not tell me how to strike such a balance. While each of us can do it for himself here and now, he finds trouble enough for himself when he includes his own future; and when we come to deal with a community, a community of say one hundred and thirty million persons, how can we possibly proceed? What we do in fact is to assume that all are alike; that what is a good for A is a good for B, and that A's preference — A's better — will be B's. Perhaps one cannot conduct a democracy on any other assumption; but not only is it not true in fact; but whatever its truth, it is impossible to make people believe it. They will do so in the abstract, but they fall into endless dispute in application, and the effort is apt to end either in mutual paralysis of action, or a seizure of power by a part. The resulting confusion and discord have therefore often suggested this solution: instill in all a faith that each achieves his personal and individual best by submerging himself in common aspirations, a common fate, a common self. There would be no denial of Liberty in that; nobody would feel himself under alien domination; each would realize himself in all, and all in each.

"Old stuff again," you will say, "it sounds good, but you know it cannot be done; people are too different, and that is all that there is to it. Once you try to make them alike you have more trouble on your hands than when you started."

On the contrary, I am disposed to believe that perhaps it can be done, for a time anyway, and for a very large proportion, at least, of a large community. Certainly I am not so sure as I used to be that it cannot be done. There are more and more signs about us that our increasingly efficient and pervasive apparatus of mass suggestion is planing off individual differences, and making us more and more facile for mass manipulation. We need not look to Russia and Germany, or to their pathetic Italian imitator; we need not leave home at all. . . . Man is a gregarious animal, extremely sensitive to authority; if it will only indoctrinate him thoroughly in his childhood and youth, he can be made to espouse any kind of orthodoxy — whether of belief or feeling. . . . And if, when we have been so "conditioned," we feel authority to be no restraint, but rather a means toward the realization of our deeper self; and if something of the sort is essential to survival in a robbers' world, where the strong are sure to win; if all these things be true, why should we boggle about any other Liberty; what more do we need? . . .

Some day such a vision may come true; the future may have in store aeons of beatitude in which men shall find utter self-realization and utter self-expression in the utter self-surrender of the hive. . . . It is not on the score of its impracticability that I do not welcome that prospect; but because I believe that its realization would suppress the most precious part of our nature. To put it very baldly, and perhaps a little contentiously, it is man's inherent willfulness that I would preserve, and in which I wish to set the stronghold of that Liberty I prize; that stone which social reformers have always rejected I would make the head of the corner.

I cannot tell why to me personally such a society seems stifling; I only know that although with Epictetus I can say: "If I were an ant, I should play the part of an ant," in fact I am not an ant, and if I try to play the part of an ant I know that I shall end in the care of a psychoanalyst. I will own that when on occasion I visit my simian cousins in captivity, the spectacle does not refresh me. Not only have they a distressing lack of reserve, but their restlessness affects me with a homeopathic uneasiness. Kipling seems right, and I wince that we have so many family traits in common. . . . Why must my cousins and I be so agitated; why this ceaseless, errant curiosity; pausing only for an instant, and then off to something new? It is all very trying; and yet here will I pitch my tent.

James Harvey Robinson used to say that we rose from the ape because like him we kept "monkeying around," always meddling with everything about us. True, there is a difference, because, although the ape meddles, he forgets, and we have learned, first to meddle and remember, and then to meddle and record. But without the meddling nothing would have happened of all that glorious array of achievement: battleships, aeroplanes, relativity, the proton, neutron and electron, T. N. T., poison gas, sulfathiozole, the Fifth Symphony, The Iliad, The Divine Comedy, Hamlet, Faust, The Critique of Pure Reason, Das Kapital, The Constitution of the United States, The Congress of Industrial Organizations, Huey Long, and The New Deal. All these from just "monkeying around"!

My thesis is that any organization of society which depresses free and spontaneous meddling is on the decline, however showy its immediate spoils; I maintain that in such a society Liberty is gone, little as its members may know it; that the Nirvana of the individual is too high a price for a collective Paradise. . . . As soon as we cease to pry about at random, we shall come to rely upon accredited bodies of authoritative dogma; and as soon as we come to rely upon accredited bodies of authoritative dogma, not only are the days of our Liberty over, but we have lost the password that has hitherto opened to us the gates of success as well. . . . Where heterodoxy in what men prize most is a crime, fresh thinking about anything will disappear. Even the loaves and fishes will not be multiplied.

As I predicted, I have brought down a very small quarry. We started to find some positive content for Liberty, and all we have discovered is that it does not follow because we are not conscious of constraint that we are not constrained. Yet little as that seems, it is not I think an altogether contemptible result, for behind it lies a faith. It is the faith that our collective fate in the end depends upon the irrepressible fertility of the individual, and the finality of what he chooses to call good. It is the faith that neither principalities, nor powers, nor things present, nor things to come, can rightfully suppress that fertility or deny that good. It is the faith in the indefectible significance of each one of us, inherited, if I understand it aright, from One who lived and died some 1900 years ago in Palestine. It is a faith not easy to live by, whose credo is full of hard sayings. If you accept it, it may cast you for the role of Prometheus, a part whose lines, you will remember, contain a good deal about defying the Powers of this World. Those powers are ruthless, competent, and strong; and among the properties in the play there are real lightning and a real eagle; make no mistake about that. Moreover, the audience is likely to be very small; indeed it is not improbable that there will be none at all. The only curtain calls you will get are those you give yourself. But the lead is a man's part, and perhaps some of us can fill it. Who can tell? . . .

IV/
Churchill as Orator
and Writer

Sir Winston Churchill (1874–1965) was educated at Harrow and Sandhurst. Unlike most statesmen, he gained renown both as orator and author. Had he been an American his oratory might well have brought him to the top long before 1940, when he first became Prime Minister in his own country. However, some degree of political unemployment enabled him to write twenty-five volumes of Churchillian history. In 1932 the literary critic Sir Herbert Read picked a paragraph from *The World Crisis* to demonstrate that Churchill's eloquence was false and artificial; "his conception of 'fine writing' is not supported by an inner structure of fine thinking. . . . the images are stale, the metaphors violent." However, after World War II, Sir Herbert admitted that Churchill had done better when "under the stress of many a great occasion his eloquence has been purified and simplified." Here we print his address to Congress of December 26, 1941; and an essay by Reed Whittemore on Churchill's history of World War II.

SIR WINSTON CHURCHILL

Address to Congress

Two weeks after Pearl Harbor, Churchill arrived at the White House, and the day after Christmas addressed Congress.* The orator himself recorded that on his return to the White House, President Roosevelt told him he "had done quite well." The understatement is doubtless Churchill's. The roars of laughter, the applause and cheers that came over the radio supported the judgment that the address had been "superbly attuned to the temper of as difficult an audience as he had ever faced."

* *Congressional Record*, Vol. 87, Pt. 9, pp. 10117–10119 (77th Congress, 1st Session) Dec. 26, 1941.

Members of the Senate and of the House of Representatives, I feel greatly honored that you should have invited me to enter the United States Senate Chamber and address the representatives of both branches of Congress.

The fact that my American forbears have for so many generations played their part in the life of the United States and that here I am, an Englishman, welcomed in your midst, makes this experience one of the most moving and thrilling in my life, which is already long and has not been entirely uneventful. [Laughter]

I wish indeed that my mother whose memory I cherish across the vale of years, could have been here to see. By the way, I cannot help reflecting that if my father had been American and my mother British, instead of the other way round, I might have got here on my own. [Laughter and applause] In that case this would not have been the first time you would have heard my voice. In that case I should not have needed any invitation; but, if I had, it is hardly likely that it would have been unanimous. [Laughter] So perhaps things are better as they are.

I may confess, however, that I do not feel quite like a fish out of water in a legislative assembly where English is spoken. I am a child of the House of Commons. I was brought up in my father's house to believe in democracy. "Trust the people" — that was his message. I used to see him cheered at meetings and in the streets by crowds of workingmen away back in those aristocratic Victorian days when, as Disraeli said, the world was for the few, and for the very few. Therefore I have been in full harmony all my life with the tides which have flowed on both sides of the Atlantic against privilege and monopoly and have steered confidently toward the Gettysburg ideal of "government of the people, by the people and for the people." [Applause]

I owe my advancement entirely to the House of Commons whose servant I am. In my country, as in yours, public men are proud to be servants of the state and would be ashamed to be its masters. On any day, if they thought the people wanted it, the House of Commons could by a simple vote remove me from my office. But I am not worrying about it at all. [Laughter] As a matter of fact, I am sure they will approve very highly of my journey here — for which I obtained the King's permission — in order to meet the President of the United States [Applause] and to arrange with him for all that mapping out of our military plans, and for all those intimate meetings of the high officers of the armed services of both countries which are indispensable to the successful prosecution of the war.

I should like to say, first of all, how much I have been impressed and encouraged by the breadth of view and sense of proportion which I have found in all quarters over here to which I have had access. Anyone who did not understand the size and solidarity of the foundations of the United States might easily have expected to find an excited, disturbed, self-centered atmosphere, with all minds fixed upon the novel, startling and painful episodes of sudden war as they hit America. After all the United States has been attacked and set upon by the three most powerfully armed dictator states, the greatest military power in Europe and the greatest military power in Asia. . . . But here in Washington, in these memorable days, I have found an Olympian fortitude which, far from being based upon complacency, is only the mask of an inflexible purpose and the proof of a sure and well-grounded confidence in the final outcome. [Applause] We in Britain had the same feeling in our darkest days. We, too, were sure that in the end all would be well.

You do not, I am certain, underrate the severity of the ordeal to which you and we have still to be subjected. The forces ranged against us are enormous; they are bitter; they are ruthless. The wicked men and their factions who have launched their peoples on the path of war and conquest know that they will be called to terrible account if they can not beat down by force of arms the peoples they have assailed. . . . They will stop at nothing that violence or treachery can suggest.

It is quite true that on our side our resources in manpower and in materials are far greater than theirs; but only a portion of your resources are as yet mobilized and developed; and we have both of us much to learn in the cruel art of war. . . .

For the best part of twenty years the youth of Britain and America have been taught that war was evil, which is true, and that it would never come again, which has been proved false.

For the best part of twenty years the youth of Germany, Japan and Italy have been taught that aggressive war is the noblest duty of the citizen, and that it should be begun as soon as the necessary weapons and organization have been made. We have performed the duties and tasks of peace. They have plotted and planned for war. This naturally has placed us in Britain, and now places you in the United States, at a disadvantage which only time, courage and straining, untiring exertions can correct.

We have indeed to be thankful that so much time has been granted to us. . . . The broad flow of munitions in Great Britain has already begun. Immense strides have been made in the conversion of American industry to military purposes. . . . Provided that every effort is made, that nothing is kept back, that the whole manpower, brainpower, virility, valor, and civic virtue of the English-speaking world, with all its galaxy of loyal, friendly or associated communities and states are bent unremittingly to the simple but supreme task, I think it would be reasonable to hope that the end of 1942 will see us quite definitely in a better position than we are now [Applause] and that the year 1943 will enable us to assume the initiative upon an ample scale. [Applause]

Some people may be startled or momentarily depressed when, like your President, I speak of a long and a hard war. Our peoples would rather know the truth, sombre though it be; and after all, when we are doing the noblest work in the world, not only defending our hearths and homes, but the cause of freedom in every land, the question of whether deliverance comes in 1942, or 1943, or 1944, falls into its proper place in the grand proportions of human history. [Applause] Sure I am that this day, now, we are the masters of our fate; that the task which has been set for us is not above our strength, and that its pangs and toils are not beyond our endurance. . . .

Not all the tidings will be evil. On the contrary, mighty strokes of war have already been dealt against the enemy. The glorious defense of their native soil by the Russian armies and people have inflicted wounds upon the Nazi tyranny and system which have bitten deep, and will fester and inflame not only in the Nazi body but in the Nazi mind [Applause] . . . .

The boastful Mussolini has crumpled already. He is now but a lackey and serf, the merest utensil of his master's will. . . . What Hitler is suffering in Libya is only a sample and a foretaste of which we must give him and his accomplices wherever this war shall lead us, in every quarter of the globe.

There are good tidings also from blue water. The life line of supplies which joins our two nations across the ocean, without which all might fail, is flowing steadily and freely, in spite of all the enemy can do. It is a fact that the British Empire, which many thought eighteen months ago was broken and ruined, is now incomparably stronger and is growing stronger with every month. [Applause]

Lastly, if you will forgive me for saying it, to me the best tiding of all, the United States, united as never before, has drawn the sword for Freedom, and cast away the scabbard. [Applause] . . .

Now that we are together, now that we are linked in a righteous comradeship of arms, now that our two considerable nations, each in perfect unity, have joined all their life energies in a common resolve, a new scene opens upon which a steady light will glow and brighten.

Many people have been astonished that Japan should, in a single day, have plunged into war against the United States and the British Empire. We all wonder why, if this dark design with all its laborious and intricate preparations, had been so long filling their secret minds, they did not choose our moment of weakness eighteen months ago. . . .

We know that for many years the policy of Japan has been dominated by secret societies of subaltern and junior officers of the Army and Navy who have enforced their will upon successive Japanese cabinets and parliaments by the assassination of any Japanese statesman who did not sufficiently further their aggressive policy. It may be that these societies, dazzled and dizzy with their own schemes of aggression and the prospect of early victories, have forced their country, against its better judgment, into war. They have certainly embarked upon a very considerable undertaking [Laughter]. . . . When we consider the resources of the United States and the British Empire, compared with those of Japan, when we remember those of China, which has so long and valiantly withstood invasion [Great applause] and when also we observe the Russian menace which hangs over Japan, it becomes still more difficult to reconcile Japan's action with prudence, or even sanity. What kind of people do they think we are? Is it possible they do not realize that we shall never cease to persevere against them until they have been taught a lesson which they and the world will never forget? [Prolonged applause]

Members of the Senate and Members of the House of Representatives, I turn for one moment more from the turmoil and convulsions of the present to the broader spaces of the future.

Here we are together, facing a group of mighty foes who seek our ruin. Here we are together, defending all that to free men is dear. Twice in a single generation the catastrophe of world war has fallen upon us; twice in our lifetimes has the long arm of Fate reached out across the oceans to bring the United States into the forefront of the battle. If we had kept together after the last war; if we had taken common measures for our safety, this renewal of the curse need never have fallen upon us [Applause].

Do we not owe it to ourselves, to our children, to tormented mankind, to make sure that these catastrophes do not engulf us for the third time?

It has been proved that pestilences may break out in the Old World which carry their destructive ravages into the New World, from which, once they are afoot, the New World cannot by any means escape. Duty and prudence alike command, first, that the germ-centres of hatred and revenge should be constantly and vigilantly surveyed and treated in good time; and, secondly, that an adequate organization should be set up to make sure that the pestilence can be controlled at its earliest beginnings before it spreads and rages throughout the entire world [Applause].

Five or six years ago it would have been easy, without shedding a drop of blood, for the United States and Great Britain to have insisted on fulfillment of the disarmament clauses of the treaties which Germany signed after the Great War. That also would have been the opportunity for assuring to Germans those raw materials which we declared in the Atlantic Charter should not be denied to any nation, victor or vanquished.

Prodigious hammer-strokes have been needed to bring us together today; or, if you will allow me to use other language, I will say that he must indeed have a blind soul who cannot see that some great purpose and design is being worked out here below, of which we have the honor to be the faithful servants.

It is not given to us to peer into the mysteries of the future; still I avow my hope and faith, sure and inviolate, that in days to come the British and American peoples will for their own safety and for the good of all, walk together side by side in majesty, in justice, and in peace. [Prolonged applause, the members of the Senate and their guests rising]

REED WHITTEMORE

Churchill as a Mythmaker

Reed Whittemore, American poet and critic, has been on the faculty of Carleton College since 1947. Born in New Haven in 1919, he was graduated from Yale in 1941, and was then a member of the American Air Force to the end of World War II. This essay, "Churchill and the Limitations of Myth," first appeared in the *Yale Review*, Winter 1954–55.*

Winston Churchill won the Nobel Prize for Literature in 1953. He won it "for his historical and biographical presentations and for the scintillating oratory in which he has stood forth as a defender of human values." The New York "Times" praised his choice editorially, adding that "words well chosen, uttered at the right time, bravely spoken, are the most powerful things in the world. They are powerful because they appeal to the hearts of men. They can drive men to madness, as Hitler's words did. They may inspire them to acts of utter heroism and self-sacrifice, as Churchill's did."

Less satisfied critics found the award merely political. They did not think with the "Times" that "the Churchill rhythm, in the highest moments of his writing or speaking, is the sound of drums and the call of trumpets"; or if they did they didn't like drums and trumpets. It was too bad, they felt, that a statesman already receiving sufficient notoriety from

* From Reed Whittemore, "Churchill and the Limitations of Myth," *Yale Review*, XLIV, pp. 248–262. Reprinted by permission of The Macmillan Co. from *The Boy From Iowa* by Reed Whittemore. Copyright 1954, 1957, 1958, 1959, 1960, 1962 by Reed Whittemore.

painting landscapes and smoking cigars had been chosen instead of a bona fide lit'ry gent.

I confess to having been on the side of the dissatisfied, though I had not at the time read the six-volume work which brought on the award. Churchill's role in the war, and his rhetoric too, were so familiar that I felt I could talk about the work without reading it, a condition I have always enjoyed. I took my cues from his most celebrated speeches. I had been in the war and carefully developed a prejudice against my platitudinous and inspirational superiors; and so far as I was concerned Churchill was the quintessence of them all.

It was therefore not a wholly generous impulse that led me later to the actual reading of "The Second World War," and I feel I should admit this right here. I should add, however, that Churchill emerged from my inquisition with, if not flying colors, at least my respect. I am now prepared to admit that he is after all a Man of Distinction (Lit'ry) and that I have in the past misjudged him. I trust he will derive comfort from my admission.

The nature of his literary talent is a matter difficult to discuss without reference to his other talents. As a leader, as a military authority, as a "naval person," and perhaps as an inventor and fair-to-middling prophet, he has demonstrated a versatility hardly to be restricted to the business of paring a paragraph or quoting (as he did before President and Mrs. Roosevelt) "Barbara Frietchie." Because he has as much right as anyone living to be admitted to Carlyle's society of Great Men, his verbal successes and defeats seem hardly worthy of discussion; one feels the obligation merely to note them and pass on to More Important Things. The Nobel Prize people presumably did this. Their award, though a literary award, was more than that, for their citation described him as "a defender of eternal human values." And the New York "Times's" approval, though having reference to the power of Churchill's words, was essentially a moral judgment, since Churchill's words were compared not with Shakespeare's or Gibbon's but with Hitler's. The comparison was surely proper. There has probably never been a literary man whose literature it is more difficult or absurd to divorce from his life.

But because this is the case one is not therefore warranted, I have discovered, in assuming that Churchill's literariness is merely a hobby with him, or a kind of gloss to his statesmanship. On the contrary, he exhibits all the rhetorical symptoms of an instructor of Freshman English. He may be writing a telegram to General Montgomery, an address to the House of Commons, or an expository account of the fall of Singapore — but whatever it is it is a literary undertaking, a labor involving cramped fingers and erasers, drafts and redrafts. This fact alone, I think, should admit him with full privileges to the literary fraternity.

Churchill's verbal interests are well attested in a single phrase in the following passage, taken from his account of the fighting with Rommel in Africa in Volume III of his "Second World War":

I brooded on the future battle in the Desert in the light of all the reports which I had studied of the spring fighting, and achieved a memorandum for the Chiefs of Staff, with the first sentence of which I was much pleased: "Renown awaits the Commander who first restores artillery to its proper place on the battlefield, from which it has been ousted by heavily armoured fighting vehicles."

I believe he was pleased with his "first sentence" because it was a kind of military prophecy; that is, Montgomery was about to demonstrate how artillery could be used effectively against armored vehicles. But I find my pleasure elsewhere; I am attracted by the curious assertion that he "*achieved* a memorandum." I wish I had had commanders who achieved memoranda rather than spewing them forth after the manner of Spenser's dragons, commanders who demonstrated a more than minimal interest in the Word. At all times Churchill did. And does. It seems to me that he can be numbered among the hordes of us who are confirmed writer-thinkers; that is, men who think by writing, who discover where they stand and what they believe and how they propose to act by putting themselves down on paper, looking at themselves there, and perhaps crossing themselves out, revising themselves, rewriting themselves interminably. They are Crocean whether they like it or not. They think in phrase and paragraph. They know with confidence only what they have expressed, and having expressed it they enjoy nothing more than rereading their achievement. For under such circumstances writing, even the writing of a memorandum, *is* an achievement.

Churchill is such a thinker, as perhaps a few examples will indicate:

In 1941 Churchill sent a memorandum to the Japanese warning them, by a series of loaded questions, against starting the war. Reading his own memorandum over several years later, he comments, "I was rather pleased with this when I wrote it, and I don't mind the look of it now."

In Canada Churchill prepared an address in which he referred to Harry Lauder as "that grand old comedian." Then on his way to give the speech he "thought of the word 'minstrel'. What an improvement. I rejoice to know that he was listening and was delighted at the reference. I am so glad I found the right word."

Just before the fall of Singapore Churchill learned for the first time that the island had no landward defenses. That it should be so incompletely defended had "no more entered my mind than that a battleship [should be] launched without a bottom." And so, like a good semanticist, he wrote off to his commander in the Far East, stating that "seaward batteries and a naval base do not constitute a fortress, which is a completely encircled strong place."

In Washington Churchill and President Roosevelt made several drafts of a statement to be made to Russia (about aid to Russia) but were unable to complete the statement before Churchill left for home by air. Churchill therefore took all the papers with him, promising to return them from Gander. Then, "as soon as we were in the air I addressed myself to the Russian communique. As I found it very hard to make head or tail of the bundle of drafts, I sent it along to General Marshall, who two hours later presented me with a typed fair copy. I was immediately impressed by this document, which exactly expressed what the President and I wanted, and did so with a clarity and comprehension not only of the military but of the political issues involved. It excited my admiration. Hitherto I had thought of Marshall as a rugged soldier and a magnificent organiser and builder of armies — the American Carnot. But now I saw he was a statesman with a penetrating and commanding view of the world scene."

In all of these passages the interest in how to say it is gratifying, but in the last passage a great deal more is involved. One can only assume that all the material Churchill and Roosevelt wished to put in their paper was present in some form in the drafts handed to General Marshall, and that Marshall's job was therefore to fuss with it until it was, in a mere verbal sense, right. Yet the results of his fussing caused Churchill suddenly to think of Marshall as a statesman. What, by these rules, is a statesman? A statesman is a gentleman who can expeditiously ("two hours later") make sense ("a typed fair copy") of a jumbled draft. A statesman is a statesman because he can express his own or others' thoughts effectively.

A prime minister who believes this about statesmanship cannot surprise us when he chides his director of military intelligence as follows: "Why must you write 'intensive' here? 'Intense' is the right word. You should see Fowler's *Modern English Usage* on the use of the two words." Nor, more important, can a prime minister who believes this escape, I think, from indulging in the weightier literary vices, if they are vices. In writing history he will inevitably follow in the footsteps of the dramatist and the poet. He will give his history a plot and a theme, and he will use his creative powers to give shape and meaning to the jumble of events he has elected to describe. He will search for imaginative rather than scientific truths.

I think Churchill is "guilty" of all this, and I wish now to discuss briefly some of the results.

"The Second World War" is an unusual mixture of history and biography. As biography it is impersonal; as history it is personal. There is very little biography except the "official" Churchill, but there is very little history except Churchill. One leaves the work with the feeling that the Second World War was after all merely an episode in the long life of this statesman.

Any history has to be written from some point of view, and for the years in question the Churchill point of view may be as sound as any. Certainly no individual was more completely immersed in the flood of events of that time than he was. And certainly Churchill is a man competent to describe them. Nonetheless the reader of this Churchillian history becomes aware very quickly that the history he is reading *is* Churchillian, and this fact about the work distinguishes it from most important histories of our time. In our time history, written history, has come to be regarded popularly as point-of-view-less. In fiction you get fiction but in history you get facts. While this view is erroneous it at least suggests what most modern historians would make of history if they could. They would like to be thought of as scholarly investigators doing their best to avoid making a merely personal construction of history. In comparison with them Churchill is a very strange scholar indeed; his sources appear to be primarily his own files; his documentary evidence was in large measure written by himself. And while the governmental position he held was so weighty as to fill his files and his own written documents with matter of indisputable historical importance, the assembling of this material in "The Second World War" inevitably makes the war a Churchill war. I do not happen to think that it was a Churchill war (though I'm prepared to acknowledge he played an important role in it), and so I am especially struck, from a literary point of view, with the achievement of Churchill in making it appear so. It seems to me — and I say this without malice — that Churchill is something of a myth-maker.

For the purposes of this essay at least the Churchill myth may be said to begin with Munich. Churchill rose to power after Munich because he had been consistently a foe of Munichs. As another historian, Cyril Falls, puts it, "Of hardly another man could it be said that his record was completely clean and satisfactory in those years when the government had been hiding its head in the sand and the opposition had been clamoring for strong action and simultaneously voting against every attempt to arm the British forces." Immediately after Munich Churchill addressed the House of Commons, saying, "This is only the first sip, the first foretaste of a bitter cup which will be proffered to us year by year unless, by a supreme recovery of moral health and martial vigour, we arise again and take our stand for freedom as in the olden time." Now politically and diplomatically Munich has become such an important symbol for the West that sixteen years later its name rings through arguments about what to do in the Far East. At least partly because of Munich, diplomatic compromises of any kind are now almost sure to be labelled "appeasement." There is no end to Munich; Munich is a modern version of the Fall of Man for most English-speaking peoples, and Churchill's statement is even now a good summary of its meaning. Several phrases in it are also a good introduction, I think, to his myth.

First, he asked for a "recovery of moral health." This I take to be his way of saying that the English after Munich had to learn all over again to recognize evil. They had lost the sense of villainy; they had no solid principles, no unshakable convictions, and so they were malleable, easily tempted to come down from the mountain. Elsewhere Churchill sustains this conviction by describing his governmental predecessors as "decided only to be undecided, resolved to be irresolute, adamant for drift." Churchill's own moral health, on the other hand, was sound as a dollar, and whenever he had occasion to describe his Nazi opponents he pulled out all the stops. Here is an example, taken from a broadcast describing the Nazi invasion of Russia:

> I see advancing . . . in hideous onslaught the Nazi war machine, with its clanking, heel-clicking, dandified Prussian officers, its crafty expert agents fresh from the cowing and tying-down of a dozen countries. I see also the dull, drilled, docile, brutish masses of the Hun soldiery plodding on like a swarm of crawling locusts. I see the German bombers and fighters in the sky, still smarting from many a British whipping, delighted to find what they believe is an easier and a safer prey.
>
> Behind all this glare, behind all this storm, I see that small group of villainous men who plan, organize and launch this cataract of horrors upon mankind.

Second, he asked for a recovery of "martial vigour." Churchill had been a staunch militarist all during the years of disarmament preceding Germany's sudden and astonishing comeback as a military power. He had seen the handwriting on the wall; he had without effect pleaded for effective action by France and England against German rearmament; and he had regularly pointed out Britain's own military weaknesses. His militarism seems to have been founded partly on his "moral health" — that is, the war against the Nazis was for him a crusade — and partly on his medieval respect for Honor. Wartime offered many fine opportunities in the honor business; it was as he said a "time when it was equally good to live or die."

Third, he asked that "we arise *again* and take our stand for freedom *as in the olden time*." Throughout "The Second World War" there are references to the olden time. When Greece was being defended against the Germans he "did not . . . give up hope of a final stand at Thermopylae. The intervening ages fell away. Why not one more undying feat of arms?" When London was being bombed the people's courage was "worthy of all that we have learned to believe of ancient Rome." When the Carlton Club in London was bombed, "Mr. Quentin Hogg . . . carried his father, a former chancellor, on his shoulders from the wreck, as Aeneas had borne Pater Anchises from the ruins of Troy." And when Churchill visited Roosevelt at the White House, "The President punctiliously made the preliminary cocktails himself, and I wheeled him in his chair from the drawing room to the lift as a mark of respect, and thinking also of Sir Walter Raleigh spreading his cloak before Queen Elizabeth." Now the flippancy of the reference to Raleigh and Pater Anchises should not be allowed to detract from the essential seriousness of the idyll of pastness that Churchill presents. In his eyes the war provided an opportunity for returning to something that had been missing in England since, say, Sir Walter Scott. It made romance real. It brought the heroic back into history. It made the mythical or ideal somehow possible again.

In summary: Churchill suggested to the English after Munich much more than that they fight the Germans. He proposed a new way of life which was a return, as he saw it, to an old way of life, a way of life that has been followed most effectively in books. As opposed to Hitler's racial power myth, with which, it seems to me, Churchill's myth has nothing at all in common, the Churchill proposals involved primarily the reassertion, not the denial, of some fine old Western ideals. "The Second World War" is his account of the success of his proposals. It therefore partakes of the qualities of the works of other mythmakers, from Homer on, even though it is disguised as "straight" history. It is history with a heroic theme, to be described as How the Good Overcame the Bad, or How the Old Virtues Prevailed.

Now central to the whole myth — and I repeat that I do not use the word "myth" maliciously — is the figure of Sir Winston Churchill himself. He is the kingpin. In his own romance he is the shining medieval hero. President Roosevelt was himself something of a hero and mythmaker and he said to Churchill once (by wire), "It is fun to be in the same decade with you." His remark seems to me to express perfectly the stature of Churchill as we see it in Churchill's own history. For Churchill is not a man to belittle his own talents. He is seldom guilty of modesty, even false modesty; of all his many admirers he has perhaps the fewest reservations about himself. And the picture that he gives us of himself in "The Second World War" is of a man who possesses all the virtues of the olden times as well as the capacity, because of his position, to do something practical with them. It was he, he advises us, who mapped the grand strategy of the war and who needled, bullied, and inspired his subordinates into carrying it out. It was he, he advises us, who kept the people's morale up during the war, who was largely responsible for the great Anglo-American alliance, and who even proposed and pushed the war's most significant tactical innovation: small, specialized invasion craft. Reading his memoranda we learn that he had his finger in everything from aircraft production to the governing of Madagascar, from the tactics for defending Tobruk to the health of Harry Hopkins. He even concerned himself with the cleaning up of a rubbish dump at Chalfont St. Giles and with ways of easing the "shoe repair situation." Our hero is courageous, prophetic, unyielding, wise, eloquent, and ubiquitous.

His heroic virtues are attached to his heroic wartime authority when he becomes Prime Minister on May 10, 1940, two years after Munich. As he himself describes it, on that date "I acquired the chief power in the State, which henceforth I wielded in ever growing measure for five years and three months, at the end of which time, all our enemies having surrendered unconditionally or being about to surrender, I was immediately dismissed by the British electorate from all further conduct of their affairs."

This passage is instructive, I think. It does not actually state that Churchill caused the unconditional surrenders, but it certainly strongly suggests it; the irony that he should be dismissed following the surrenders is hardly meaningful unless much responsibility for the surrenders is his. Now if the passage were an isolated instance I could dismiss it as merely a careless statement in which two unrelated matters are juxtaposed. It isn't an isolated instance. Throughout the work the activities of all the English and of Churchill are similarly merged; the difference between "we" and "I" is not insisted upon. The result is that for the duration of what I call the myth our hero appears like a sovereign in a Shakespeare play who, with a few noble lords around him, personally triumphs over the enemy. And when the myth ends — it ends when he is relieved of his office in August of 1945 — so also does the order and unanimity of purpose among the Allies which prevailed during Churchill's rule. Remembering Churchill's lonely stand against the policies which brought about Munich, I find it significant that the theme of the final volume of his work is "How the Great Democracies Triumphed, and so Were able to *Resume* the Follies Which Had so Nearly Cost Them Their Life." That is, the course of democratic folly is the normal course, but for the heroic period of Churchill's rule democracy outdid itself.

I am reminded of Carlyle's statement: "The history of all rebellions is that you have put the *Un*able Man at the head of affairs . . . find me a King, or Able Man, and he has a divine right over me." Substitute "follies" for "rebellions" and the parallel is clear. Certainly Churchill regards himself as the Able Man, and though he is not King he doesn't let that slight oversight by destiny worry him much. In fact he is sometimes a bit patronizing to his King: "I have been greatly cheered by our weekly luncheons in poor old bomb-battered Buckingham Palace."

This is nothing compared to his treatment of other people's kings. Then he is positively paternal. He advises the Emperor of Ethiopia how the Emperor should regard his restoration, by the English, to the throne: "Your Majesty was the first of the lawful sovereigns to be driven from his throne and country by the Fascist-Nazi criminals, and you are now the first to return in triumph." (The point is that it's really a British, or Churchill, triumph.) He informs the King of Greece that he has "a great opportunity of leaving a name in history"; and he tells the premier of Yugoslavia that "your excellency may rise to the height of world events." This is all pure royal condescension surely, with Churchill as the royalty.

Our hero, then, is more than just an ordinary run-of-the-mill hero "with a lance upon a rack, . . . a lean horse, and a greyhound." He is also a benevolent democratic despot (if there is such a thing), a latter-day Henry V. When he walks amid the ruins of London the bomb-battered inhabitants wipe away their tears and cheer wildly. It is true that as he describes it they cheer wildly not for Winnie but for "King and Country"; but the occasion for cheering is indisputably Winnie, a little touch of Winnie in the night. Under such circumstances he can hardly avoid thinking of his role in the war with considerable egotism, or avoid regarding the war at times as his own private affair. Thus he tells us that "I did not myself at all shrink mentally from the impending [battle of Britain]," that "I felt acutely the need of Pantellaria," and that "this mortal danger to our life-lines [U-Boats] gnawed my bowels." We see him, after a British defeat in Africa, wandering about his country estate "disconsolately for hours." And we learn that the campaign in Burma did not appeal to him because, among other things, "I hated jungles."

Also private in nature, because Churchill is running them, are Britain's relations with her allies. Particularly intimate are the meetings between Churchill and Roosevelt, where they carve the world up over cocktails (mixed personally by the President) and stay up late together correcting the phrasing of the Atlantic Charter or of a titanic memorandum to co-hero Stalin. They also relax together — for all work and no play would make the Grand Alliance a dull boy. They ride up to Shangri-La reciting "Barbara Frietchie" and go dashing off to Marrakech to see a sunset.

Between Stalin and Churchill there is no recorded communion about sunsets, but the grand informality of the great with the great continues. Churchill describes for Stalin the proposed Western strategy of a double front by drawing a quick picture of a crocodile and then, simply, explaining "our intention to attack the soft belly of the crocodile as we [attack] his hard snout." Could there be higher strategy than this, two great leaders seated at a table together analyzing the fate of Europe by reference to a crude drawing of a crocodile? And after the business of the day has been transacted there is of course relaxation; on one such occasion Stalin goes around the dinner table collecting autographs and then Churchill and Stalin drink to each other:

> I filled a small-sized claret glass with brandy for him and another for myself. I looked at him significantly. We both drained our glasses at a stroke and gazed approvingly at one another. After a pause Stalin said, "If you find it impossible to give us a fortified position in the Marmora, could we not have a base at Dedeagatch?" I contented myself with saying, "I will always support Russia in her claim to the freedom of the seas all year round."

This passage has, I think, most of the mythic elements I have been discussing. As in a Western movie the two heroes appraise each other narrowly over a drink, each finding the other formidable and each enjoying the discovery because, out where men are men or up where leaders are titans, one chooses one's opponents carefully; it would be weak and dishonorable for a genuine hero to come to words or blows with anyone of less heroic stature than himself. So, having looked at each other for appraisal purposes, and having drained their glasses to give their wondering audience a foretaste of their prowess, they acknowledge with an almost imperceptible smile the other's worthiness and get down to business. In a Western they would now sit down at the poker table, but in diplomacy the stakes are not chips but territory; so they begin to maneuver for an advantageous position, talking as I imagine it in an emotionless monotone with their eyes lazily half-closed and their bodies wholly relaxed (though each is fast as lightning on the draw), and perhaps leaning casually on the bar. Stalin says, "If you find it impossible to give us a fortified position in the Marmora, could we not have a base at Dedeagatch?" [1] Churchill replies evenly, and without moving a muscle or giving away one inch of Dedeagatch (he is generous, large-hearted, but above all unyielding), "I will always support Russia in her claim to freedom of the seas all year round." The scene might have been better if he had replied, evenly of course, that he would be pleased to exchange a base at Dedeagatch for a base at Vladivostok; but it is pretty good as it is.

Faced with such evidence of Churchill's legendary person, I confess that many of the genuinely legendary persons I am familiar with seem a bit frail and impotent. They have most of Churchill's virtues perhaps, but they haven't the world to display them in. Churchill has. From Marrakech to Singapore, and from Washington to Melbourne his rule extends, and he rules not merely land but air and sea as well. He has also one

---

[1] Dedeagatch, or Alexandroupolis, is a port in eastern Greece.

other quality not shared by many of his fellow princes, potentates, thrones, and imperial powers. He is indomitable.

Almost everyone who has written about Churchill, including Churchill, has said that he is indomitable. He is "an ever-fixed mark that looks on tempests and is never shaken." He is a rock. Nothing moves him except time and bad health and the British electorate (the electorate moved him in August of 1945); he seems to be immune to the other elements. And so he does not have to worry, as the old heroes had to, about the whims of the gods. The British electorate gives him a much freer heroic hand than a fickle Athene or Poseidon ever would have, with the result that he is, while he is running things, always optimistic, always confident that things will come out right. Except for one weak moment, previously mentioned, when he was disconsolate at his country estate following a defeat in Africa, he is buoyant and imperturbable in the face of the most severe disasters. He is thus never guilty of the weakness the old heroes displayed in their laments when they sat on a rock and bewailed their birth, upbringing, and subsequent unrelieved misfortune. I suspect that Poseidon and Athene should regard themselves as lucky they never had to tackle this man. They might have fared as badly as Hitler did, Hitler to whom Churchill referred whimsically as "the gent" and "that man" and "that bad man," adding that "in his heart he was one of our admirers."

It is important — and especially important for a literary man — to believe that the relationship between history and myth is an amicable one. A literary man has to have something to say about the truth of myth or he will have trouble defending his profession. This is therefore what I have to say about it. It seems to me that a great deal of reasonably sound history can be and has been written by reducing the activities of whole nations or peoples or groups to the negotiable activities of a select few, and that such reduction or simplification is an honest form of mythologizing so long as the select few are representative of — and may therefore qualify as symbols of — the groups out of which they have somehow or other been strained. When, accordingly, Churchill says that he "had the honour to *express* . . . the buoyant and imperturbable temper of Britain," he seems to me to be acknowledging his role in this kind of mythologizing process, acknowledging, that is, that he was primarily Britain's agent, not an independent and unpredictable individual running a business of his own.

The difficulty I have at this point, however, is that Churchill's role seems to be really other than and greater than that of merely expressing the British people's temper. His heroics make him more than the people's symbol; they make him superior to the people; they make him their thoroughgoing leader, a man who in a very positive sense controls the people's destiny. Now leading is very different from representing, and

11690

the mythologizing of leaders is a much more difficult historical procedure to defend these days than it used to be. It was all right for Shakespeare to have Henry V swing the tide of battle at Agincourt with his brave words about St. Crispin's Day, but it seems somewhat arrogant of Churchill to say in North Africa that "it gave me intense pleasure to see my great colleague [Roosevelt] here on conquered or liberated territory which *he and I had secured* . . . [my italics]." I happen personally to have been in North Africa about this time, and while I don't claim to have secured the place I question the justice of Churchill's claiming to have done so. And though I am not English I similarly question Churchill's announcement that, having been asked by the English people to "Give it 'em back" (give back to the Germans their bombings), he personally "undertook forthwith to see that their wishes were carried out; and this promise was certainly kept."

To summarize my difficulty, I can accept the thesis, partly because it is an ancient one, that Henry V, who was personally on the field at Agincourt, had much to do with the English victory there; but I can't accept the thesis that Churchill, by writing memoranda to the Air Ministry and Roosevelt, gave a single bomb back to, or secured a single alien province from, anybody. At this point the myth loses my allegiance.

I think the difficulty arises partly from Churchill's writing about himself. Mythologizing seems not just egotistical under such circumstances; it seems also delusive. "Human kind," says Eliot, "cannot bear very much reality." One reality, however, that seems to me must be borne is the smallness, the limited scope of self. One may in imagination lend a great deal of authority and virtue and prowess to others without being personally deluded; it is not just an act of faith; it is an act of creation like sculpturing an enormous figure for some garden. When complete the piece exists in its own odd right outside the self, an ideal if you will, or a projection of possibilities. But to let the imagination go to work on oneself, to lend the self all the authority and virtue and prowess that imagination can conceive — this, it seems to me, is a real evasion of the reality of self. To put it grossly, how can poor forked Churchill, as he pulls on his trousers in the morning, say that he secured North Africa?

Few of us have the grand opportunity for self-delusion that fate has afforded Churchill, and his delusion here, if I am correct, is surely understandable. Furthermore, in Churchill's defense, the obvious should be pointed out, that his record as a prophet shows him to be among the least deluded of men so far as the "outside" world is concerned. I am glad to report therefore that I think the primary difficulty with his history of the war is not this — that is, it is not that Churchill is writing about Churchill — but that the myth he presents to us is so extensive. There seems to be a variable limit to myth; myth works on a sliding scale.

In a myth-favoring age it works fine right out to the end where, I imagine, sit characters like King Arthur and Miss Weston; but in a period like our own, or at least among persons who share my cynical incredulities, it can only go to that point beyond "facts" where it still looks like "facts." Churchill goes beyond that point. Remembering (imperfectly, I think) his compliment to the RAF, that never have so many owed so much to so few, I suggest that the real few of his myth are the following: Churchill, General Montgomery, General Wavell, General Eisenhower, Stalin, Roosevelt, and perhaps again Churchill. This is too few for me.

This may also be too few for a good many admirers of Churchill's history, who will point out how much of it is not about these few but about the Allies in general, and who will add that the bulk of it is not, as I have indicated, personal and self-approving but of a relatively objective, expository nature. I agree that I have suggested that myth plays a larger part in the work than, in bulk, it does, and I apologize for my fault. I think, however, that if anything the objectivity of the largest sections of the work serves to enlarge rather than to diminish the scope of the myth. For the myth, being superimposed upon what purports to be a very full account of the whole war, becomes insensibly a part of the whole war. Here is a final example.

Churchill reports that he made a tour of the Normandy front after "General Montgomery reported that he was sufficiently established ashore to receive a visit." In his description of his private tour he does not say that he had any influence upon the maneuvers of the armies in the field. Furthermore, his tour is not a significant one in isolation; a good many newspaper correspondents and other uninvolved personnel of great wisdom made similar tours. But in the context of the myth, with the whole background present of Churchill's memoranda on how the landings might best be effected, the tour seems to be more than a tour; it appears as yet another instance of the long arm of our hero in the making of history. On top of this, in the statement that "General Montgomery reported that he was sufficiently established ashore to receive a visit," I find no mention of General Montgomery's army. The omission is unimportant perhaps; neither Churchill nor Montgomery would have wished the army slighted; but it is still another indication of the presence of the myth, here working without show and without pomp presiding.

V / Modes of Denunciation

Denunciation is a broader term than censure, defamation or vilification, but like them it is a serviceable political weapon which has not been threatened by modern technology. Here are several examples of American denunciation from Capitol Hill which have not been denatured by senatorial courtesy.

THOMAS CONNOLLY AND CARTER GLASS

The Censure of Senator Nye

In the mid-thirties Senator Gerald P. Nye of North Dakota directed a prolonged munitions inquiry relating to our entry into World War I. One day he released evidence that President Wilson had known about the Allies' secret treaties almost two years earlier than Wilson himself stated in 1919. When the headlines on January 16, 1936, credited Nye with branding Wilson a liar, Senators Tom Connolly of Texas and Carter Glass of Virginia defended President Wilson by vigorously attacking Senator Nye.*

MR. CONNOLLY. Mr. President, for some time I have observed the course of the Munitions Committee with a great deal of interest and frequently with amazement; but not until today, with the appearance in the press of the charges by the Senator from North Dakota (Mr. Nye) attacking very courageously and bravely two men who are now dead, did the operations of this committee reach what I believe to be their, so far, lowest depth of performance. . . .

Mr. President, I was not an intimate of President Woodrow Wilson. I was only a new member of the House of Representatives when the war began; but, without that intimacy I, as one of his admirers . . . desire to express my own resentment of the coarse, common insult which the

* *Congressional Record,* Vol. 80, Pt. 1, pp. 501–2, 572–3 (Jan. 16, 17, 1936).

69

Senator from North Dakota has heaped upon one of the great figures
in American history.

I am not speaking as a Democrat. Let us for the moment forget par-
tisanship. Whether you loved Woodrow Wilson or whether you hated
him, whether you agreed with him or whether you opposed him, when
the history of this Republic shall be written his titanic figure will tower
above some of the puny pigmies who now bark at his memory as Pike's
Peak towers above the fog and the bog of that Arkansas swamp which
only yesterday engulfed seventeen human lives.

Mr. President, being one who is devoted to parliamentary ethics and
parliamentary observance, and one of limited resources, I find it very
difficult to find language adequate to express my contempt for efforts of
this kind to besmirch the memory of the man Woodrow Wilson whose
tongue is now silent. . . .

If the Senator from North Dakota is so heroic — this white knight of
peace — if he wants to make charges like this, why does he not single
out some double-fisted man who is still alive. There are many in this
body, and many elsewhere in Washington, who had a part in the
transactions to which he has referred, and let him impugn their purposes
and their motives. . . . Some checker-playing, beer-drinking, back room
of some low house is the only place fit for the kind of language which
the Senator from North Dakota, the Chairman of the Committee, this
Senator who is going to lead us out toward peace, puts into the Record
about a dead man, a great man, a good man, and a man who when alive
had the courage to meet his enemies face to face and eye to eye. No
one ever saw Woodrow Wilson sheathe his sword so long as combat was
on.

MR. GLASS. Mr. President, it is with great reluctance that I
venture to trespass upon the time of the Senate today [but] it occurred
to me, and the thought was confirmed by suggestions from my colleagues,
that, as a more or less intimate friend of the late Woodrow Wilson and
as a former member of his official family, it would be pertinent if I
should briefly respond to the shocking assault made upon his character
and the attempted impeachment of his integrity and his veracity. This
I shall do in unmistakable terms and, but for the limitations of the rules
of the Senate, in phraseology which I am not accustomed to use.

If it were permissible in the Senate to say that any man who would
asperse the integrity and veracity of Woodrow Wilson is a coward, if it
were permissible to say that his charge is not only malicious but positively
mendacious, that I would be glad to say here or elsewhere to any man,
whether he be a United States Senator or not, because the charge would
be not only destitute of decency but it would be such a shocking exhibi-

tion as never has happened in the thirty-five years I have served in the Congress of the United States. In that period no President of the United States, however bitter his adversaries, has ever been charged on the floor of the Senate with having deliberately falsified in a matter of importance. . . .

From time to time it has been suggested in the newspapers that the members of the committee were going to present to the country shocking revelations. It remained until day before yesterday to present anything of a shocking nature; and that was the unspeakable accusation made against a dead President — dirt-daubing the sepulchre of Woodrow Wilson. . . .

Now Mr. President lest I should infringe those rules which I always obey, perhaps I should better desist, because what I feel like saying here or elsewhere to the man who thus insults the memory of Woodrow Wilson is something which may not be spoken here, or printed in the newspapers, or uttered by a gentleman [applause].

WAYNE MORSE

The Verbiage of Defense and Attack

Over-extended sessions of Congress encourage even Senators to play games with personal invective. In November, 1963, Senator Everett Dirksen of Illinois mimicked and ridiculed Senator Wayne Morse of Oregon for his delaying tactics on the Foreign Aid bill. When Morse returned to the Chamber it was his turn.*

MR. MORSE. Mr. President, I understand that while I was out of the Chamber this afternoon, presiding as chairman of the Senate conferees on the higher education bill, the Senator from Illinois (Mr. Dirksen) discussed the motion of the senior Senator from Oregon [Mr. Morse] to recommit the foreign aid bill to committee and, in the opinion of colleagues, paid his disrespects in sarcasm and ridicule to the senior Senator from Oregon.

I judge from what I have heard that the speech of the Senator from Illinois shows that he and I have nothing in common. I am glad, if that is true, that it does, because I would never want to be that common. I am delighted to know that I no longer belong to a political party so bankrupt in leadership that it is dependent upon the alleged leadership of the Senator from Illinois.

* *Congressional Record,* Vol. 109, pp. 19865–6 (Nov. 1, 1963).

I understand that the speech was characterized by ill manners and bad taste. But I am accustomed to that from the Senator from Illinois.

I am very proud of the fact that I have never won his good will; because if I did, I would have to engage in some very long introspection. . . . I take this as one of the normal courses of events that sometimes take place in the Senate, when Senators are so lacking in their facts that they have to resort to ridicule, personal sarcasm, and personal abuse as a substitute for logic, reason, and evidence.

*   *   *

Two weeks later Senator Morse was attacked by the columnist, Joseph Alsop, for seeking to delay and gut the foreign aid bill. In the piece, entitled "The New Know-Nothings," Alsop referred to Morse as "the Oregon paragon," and described him as "ineffable." Senator Morse's rejoinder was immediate.*

MR. MORSE. Mr. President, in this morning's Washington Post, an alleged newspaperman by the name of Joseph Alsop has published a scathing criticism of the Senate opponents of the wasteful, inefficient, and corruption-producing foreign aid program of the administration and the Foreign Relations Committee.

This is the Alsop who is the well-known lackey of the Pentagon Building and the State Department. His war-mongering columns for a long time past have demonstrated his disregard for, and presumably his ignorance of, the checks and balances system provided by our constitutional fathers and indelibly written into the Constitution itself.

His writings give the impression that he would be happier if the President of the United States were given dictatorial powers similar to those of many of the Fascist leaders of the world whose regimes Alsop seems to admire so much.

He gives the impression that he would like to be an intellectual snob, but lacks the intellect to be snobbish about.

I am very proud of my enemies, particularly the members of the yellow press; and I am highly complimented to have this gutter journalist confess his enmity to me in his irrational, White House bootlicking column of this morning.

I ask unanimous consent that his column entitled, "The New Know-Nothings," be printed in the Record, inasmuch as it is such devastating proof of his own know-nothingism.[1]

* *Congressional Record*, Vol. 109, pp. 20843–4 (Nov. 15, 1963).
[1] Mr. Alsop has expressed his regret at being unable to give permission to reprint his column here.

VI/The Oratory of Civil Rights

RICHARD RUSSELL AND PAUL DOUGLAS

The Pro's and Con's of Civil Rights

In June 1963 President Kennedy strongly urged civil rights legislation in a message to Congress and a television appeal to the nation. Here are two contrasting reactions in the Senate followed by the Rev. Martin Luther King's moving speech at the Lincoln Memorial two months later. Senator Richard Russell of Georgia was born at Winder, Georgia, in 1897, was educated at Gordon Institute and the University of Georgia. Senator Paul Douglas of Illinois was born at Salem, Massachusetts, in 1892; was educated at Bowdoin and Columbia, and taught at Chicago before entering politics in 1937. Both Senators are Democrats.

MR. RUSSELL. Mr. President, the President's speech appealed eloquently to the emotions but completely disregarded reason, human experience, and true equality under the Constitution.*

The fact that every citizen has the same right to own and operate a swimming pool or dining hall constitutes equality. The use of Federal power to force the owner of a dining hall or swimming pool to unwillingly accept those of a different race as guests creates a new and special right for Negroes in derogation of the property rights of all of our people to own and control the fruits of their labor and ingenuity.

The outstanding distinction between a government of free men and a socialistic or communistic state is the fact that free men can own and control property, whereas statism denies property rights.

The phrase "from each according to his ability and to each according to his need" may have greater emotional appeal than "work hard to acquire property and the law will protect you in its enjoyment." However,

* From the *Congressional Record*, Vol. 109, p. 10323 (June 17, 1963).

Marxism has not worked and can never work because it does not take human nature into account. To rebut the emotional appeal, we have the hard, undeniable fact that in our free enterprise system we have plenty, whereas the Marxists — though they have never been able to apply literally their avowed creed — all suffer from scarcity and privation.

Our American system has always rejected the idea that one group of citizens may deprive another of legal rights in property by process of agitation, demonstration, intimidation, law defiance, and civil disobedience.

I do not believe that the American people will be easily frightened into discarding our system for adventures into socialism that have been discredited wherever tried.

The highest office of the land should symbolize respect for law, whether it be legally enacted ordinances of the meanest hamlet in the land or the written word of our national charter — the Constitution.

I was, therefore, shocked to hear the President justify, if not encourage, the present wave of mass demonstrations accompanied by the practices of sitting or lying in public streets and blocking traffic; forming human walls before the doors of legal businesses and assaulting with deadly weapons officers of the law whose only offense was undertaking to maintain order and protect private property.

The South has its shortcomings as well as other areas. But a calculated campaign waged by the metropolitan press, television and radio, has magnified the unfortunate occurrences in the South while crimes of violence in other areas have been minimized. This has generated bitterness and hatred against the white people of the Southern States almost amounting to a national disease. It is also encouraging a condition bordering on anarchy in many communities. These terrible conditions are sure to further deteriorate with increasing disorder unless the President of the United States desists from using threats of mass violence to rush his social equality legislation through the Congress.

No American citizen has the right to select the laws he will obey and those he will disobey.

The President of the United States has a higher call to leadership, than to use threats of mass violence and disregard of reasonable local laws as a means of securing action in the courts and Congress, however desirable he may regard it to be.

The Congress of the United States, by an enactment of March 1, 1875, declared that all persons were entitled "to the full and equal enjoyment of the accommodations, advantages, facilities, and privileges of inns, public conveyances on land or water, theaters, and other places of public amusement." The Supreme Court of the United States on October 15, 1883, declared this Federal restriction upon the use and control of private property to be unconstitutional.

When white citizens protest against the Supreme Court decision in the school cases, they are immediately told that those decisions are the "law of the land" and that, if they protest too vigorously or violently, the armed might of the United States will be summoned to subdue them. Our Negro citizens, who are conducting daily demonstrations against the "law of the land" as established by the Supreme Court in the civil rights cases in 1883, are encouraged to increase the velocity of their demonstrations by the belief that the Attorney General, the FBI, the hundreds of U. S. marshals, and the Armed Forces of the United States will protect them in their demonstrations. The President of the United States cites these demonstrations as reasons for a legislative stampede to change this "law of the land." All this in the name of American equality and justice.

The President and the Attorney General now say that they will predicate this new thrust for race mixing on the already tortured commerce clause of the Constitution. If the commerce clause will sustain an act to compel the white owner of a dining hall to accept a Negro against his wishes, it can be used to sustain the validity of legislation that will compel his admittance into the living room or bedroom of any citizen.

I believe in equality before the law for every American. In equal measure, I reject the idea that Federal power may be invoked to compel the mingling of the races in social activities to achieve the nebulous aim of social equality.

Every Negro citizen possesses every legal right that is possessed by any white citizen, but there is nothing in either the Constitution or Judaeo-Christian principles or commonsense and reason which would compel one citizen to share his rights with one of another race at the same place and at the same time. Such compulsion would amount to a complete denial of the inalienable rights of the individual to choose or select his associates.

I hope that the American people will not be swept further down the road to socialism by the present unprecedented wave of propaganda. To me, the President's legislative proposals are clearly destructive of the American system and the constitutional rights of American citizens. I shall oppose them with every means and resource at my command. I do not believe a majority of the Congress will be frightened by thinly veiled threats of violence.

MR. DOUGLAS. As in the past, Senators who believe in a genuine civil rights measure will probably be very lonely as we work here on the Senate floor.* I hope there may have been a sufficient change in public opinion and a sufficient realization of the severity of the issue, so that the precedents of the past will no longer apply to the future.

* From the *Congressional Record*, Vol. 109, p. 10548 (June 19, 1963).

I pride myself on being not only an advocate of civil rights, but also on being a realist with an understanding of some of the difficulties which we face. As such difficulties develop, there will be those who will say, . . . "Eliminate the provisions on public accommodations. Then we can get an antifilibuster vote, but you never can get it as long as you keep the public accommodations section in the bill." I only hope that the strange combinations of sponsorships which have been revealed today are not harbingers of such tactics.

When that section is thrown overboard it will then be said, "We can get the bill through provided you eliminate the fair and full employment practices provision" — just as the provisions, under equity proceedings, for punishing violations of injunctions were thrown out in 1957 under the plea that our southern friends and their sympathizers would never consent to that.

Then there will be the cry, "Eliminate part III. Eliminate the right of the Attorney General, in school desegregation cases, to intervene. You never can get by with that."

So gradually movements will be made to strip the bill of all meaning, with the final result that a bill may emerge that will be completely innocuous and completely ineffective. And then it will be hailed by some as a great victory for civil rights.

It might have been possible to get by with that in 1957 and 1959, but I do not think it is possible today, because what the leadership's dealing with now is not merely a group of liberals in the Senate. What they are dealing with now is the alarmed and deeply concerned public opinion of the vast majority of the Nation; and the little parliamentary tricks and devices, the backroom whisperings, and the cloakroom deals will not be effective in meeting this situation out in the country.

What we need is a stern determination. We are encompassed by opponents. We are encompassed by persons who will try to rob this measure of all real meaning. We must be faithful to the principles, work for the President's program and resist all the efforts and blandishments to emasculate the measure.

We will debate without bitterness, without malice, without any false sense of sectional superiority, but some of us, at least, will insist that the principles of the Declaration of Independence and of the 14th and 15th amendments to the Constitution be applied all over the Nation. And in this we are not disturbers, nor are we, as some columnists have said, "knee-jerk liberals."

We believe in the rights of man. We believe in the eternal principles upon which this Republic was founded. Since when are those principles to be sneered at?

I am not too optimistic about the outcome, but if we fail, if either no bill or a badly emasculated bill emerges, it will be a great blow inside the Nation to the cause of righteousness. It will be a great blow to the standing of the United States in the public opinion of the world. If we go on month after month with a filibuster and a progressive whittling down of the program, we shall make ourselves not only ridiculous, but despicable, in the sight of the whole world. Our enemies will take full advantage of that fact.

American prestige will be lowered. We must make the decision. Do we believe in Thomas Jefferson's preamble to the Declaration of Independence:

> We hold these truths to be self-evident, that all men are created equal, that they are endowed by their Creator with certain unalienable rights, that among these are life, liberty and the pursuit of happiness. That to secure these rights, Governments are instituted among Men, deriving their just powers from the consent of the governed,

Do we believe in Lincoln's Gettysburg Address, that this is a government not only of the people, by the people and for the people? Do we believe in the 14th amendment to the Constitution, which provides that no State shall deprive any citizen of the equal protection of the laws; that all persons born or naturalized in the United States are not only citizens of a particular State but also citizens of the United States, and that no person shall be deprived of life, liberty, or property without due process of law? There is no room for second-class citizenship under the 14th amendment.

These are things we talk about on the Fourth of July. These are subjects for orations. However, do we really believe in these principles? The test is coming. We must stand fast behind the program which the President of the United States has laid down, resist the processes of erosion which inevitably will be employed, and answer quorum calls, even to the point of dropping from fatigue. Without indulging in mock heroics, it may be from something else than fatigue.

We must do this without bitterness or any irritating air of moral superiority. We recognize that our Southern friends — and they are our friends — are in fact prisoners of history and geography, and that an evil system was fastened upon them — slavery — which was bad and terrible for the slave, and bad and terrible for the master. When the slaves were freed, the social conditions which had prevailed under slavery continued, and they poisoned the life of the South and the life of the North.

Now at a tardy hour we are seeking to make atonement. Therefore, I wish to commend the President of the United States for his brave and sweeping and comprehensive message.

I pray to God that in the difficult months which are to follow we will resist the temptations of expediency and seek to do what is right, and to remember the hymn of Isaac Watts, which we used to sing in Sunday School and church:

> Tasks in hours of insight willed
> May be in hours of gloom fulfilled.

The hours of gloom will soon set upon us. I hope that the inspiration of this hour, the stirring words of our President, may be carried out in the months of gloom which I fear lie ahead.

MARTIN LUTHER KING

I Have a Dream

Popular support for civil rights for the Negro came to a climax in a massive march on Washington on August 28, 1963. Late in the lengthy program of speeches and song at the Lincoln Memorial, Martin Luther King delivered this deeply moving address.* Dr. King was born in Atlanta, Georgia, in 1929, and educated at Morehouse and Boston University. A Baptist minister, founder and president of the Southern Christian Leadership Conference, he has been an indefatigable crusader for civil rights for the Negro.

Now is the time to make real the promises of democracy. Now is the time to rise from the dark and desolate valley of segregation to the sunlit path of racial justice. Now is the time to lift our nation from the quicksands of racial injustice to the solid rock of brotherhood. Now is the time to make justice a reality for all of God's children.

There will be neither rest nor tranquillity in America until the Negro is granted his citizenship rights. The whirlwinds of revolt will continue to shake the foundations of our nation until the bright day of justice emerges.

And that is something that I must say to my people who stand on the threshold which leads to the palace of justice. In the process of gaining our rightful place we must not be guilty of wrongful deeds.

Again and again, we must rise to the majestic heights of meeting physical force with soul force. The marvelous new militancy which has engulfed the Negro community must not lead us to a distrust of all white people, for many of our white brothers as evidenced by their presence here today have come to realize that their destiny is tied up with our destiny!

* From the *New York Times*, Aug. 29, 1963. Copyright © 1963 by Martin Luther King, Jr, Reprinted by permission of Joan Daves.

There are those who are asking the devotees of civil rights, "When will you be satisfied?" We can never be satisfied as long as the Negro is the victim of the unspeakable horrors of police brutality. We can never be satisfied as long as our bodies, heavy with the fatigue of travel, cannot gain lodging in the motels of the highways and the hotels of the cities.

We can never be satisfied as long as our children are stripped of their selfhood and robbed of their dignity by signs stating "for whites only." We cannot be satisfied as long as the Negro in Mississippi cannot vote and the Negro in New York believes he has nothing for which to vote.

No, we are not satisfied and we will not be satisfied until justice rolls down like water and righteousness like a mighty stream.

Now, I am not unmindful that some of you have come here out of great trials and tribulations. Some of you have come fresh from narrow jail cells.

Continue to work with the faith that honor in suffering is redemptive. Go back to Mississippi, go back to Alabama, go back to South Carolina, go back to Georgia, go back to Louisiana, go back to the slums and ghettos of our Northern cities, knowing that somehow this situation can and will be changed. Let us not wallow in the valley of despair.

Now, I say to you today, my friends, so even though we face the difficulties of today and tomorrow, I still have a dream. It is a dream deeply rooted in the American dream. I have a dream that one day this nation will rise up and live out the true meaning of its creed: "We hold these truths to be self-evident, that all men are created equal."

I have a dream that one day on the red hills of Georgia the sons of former slaves and the sons of former slave-owners will be able to sit down together at the table of brotherhood.

I have a dream that one day even the state of Mississippi, a state sweltering with the people's injustice, sweltering with the heat of oppression, will be transformed into an oasis of freedom and justice.

I have a dream that my four little children will one day live in a nation where they will not be judged by the color of their skin, but by the content of their character.

This is our hope. This is the faith that I go back to the South with — with this faith we will be able to hew out of the mountain of despair a stone of hope.

VII / Presidential Styles

Political prose is most ceremonial in the inaugural addresses of our presidents. Combining in some proportion what the new (or re-elected) president has to say, and what he believes the nation wants and expects to hear, the inaugural address repays the closest study for message and style. Ideally it relates the present with a worthy past, appeals for unity and dedication, and offers a formulation of national purpose and goals. Here we reprint Lincoln's inaugural of 1865 and President Kennedy's of 1961.

ABRAHAM LINCOLN

With Malice Toward None

When Lincoln was inaugurated the second time, six weeks before his assassination, the Civil War was nearing the end, and the President was deeply absorbed in the significance of the costly struggle and the possibility of reconciliation and reunion. The date was March 4, 1865.*

Fellow-Countrymen: At this second appearing to take the oath of the Presidential office there is less occasion for an extended address than there was at the first. Then a statement somewhat in detail of a course to be pursued seemed fitting and proper. Now, at the expiration of four years, during which public declarations have been constantly called forth on every point and phase of the great contest which still absorbs the attention and engrosses the energies of the nation, little that is new could be presented. The progress of our arms, upon which all else chiefly depends, is as well known to the public as to myself, and it is, I trust, reasonably satisfactory and encouraging to all. With high hope for the future, no prediction in regard to it is ventured.

* From James D. Richardson, ed., *Messages and Papers of the Presidents, 1789–1905* (Washington, 1907) VI. 276–77.

On the occasion corresponding to this four years ago all thoughts were anxiously directed to an impending civil war. All dreaded it, all sought to avert it. While the inaugural address was being delivered from this place, devoted altogether to *saving* the Union without war, insurgent agents were in the city seeking to *destroy* it without war — seeking to dissolve the Union and divide effects by negotiation. Both parties deprecated war, but one of them would *make* war rather than let the nation survive, and the other would *accept* war rather than let it perish, and the war came.

One eighth of the whole population was colored slaves, not distributed generally over the Union, but localized in the southern part of it. These slaves constituted a peculiar and powerful interest. All knew that this interest was somehow the cause of the war. To strengthen, perpetuate, and extend this interest was the object for which the insurgents would rend the Union even by war, while the Government claimed no right to do more than to restrict the territorial enlargement of it. Neither party expected for the war the magnitude or the duration which it has already attained. Neither anticipated that the *cause* of the conflict might cease with or even before the conflict itself should cease. Each looked for an easier triumph, and a result less fundamental and astounding. Both read the same Bible and pray to the same God, and each invokes His aid against the other. It may seem strange that any men should dare to ask a just God's assistance in wringing their bread from the sweat of other men's faces, but let us judge not, that we be not judged. The prayers of both could not be answered. That of neither has been answered fully. The Almighty has His own purposes. "Woe unto the world because of offenses; for it must needs be that offenses come, but woe to that man by whom the offense cometh." If we shall suppose that American slavery is one of those offenses which, in the providence of God, must needs come, but which, having continued through His appointed time, He now wills to remove, and that He gives to both North and South this terrible war as the woe due to those by whom the offense came, shall we discern therein any departure from those divine attributes which the believers in a living God always ascribe to Him? Fondly do we hope, fervently do we pray, that this mighty scourge of war may speedily pass away. Yet, if God wills that it continue until all the wealth piled by the bondsman's two hundred and fifty years of unrequited toil shall be sunk, and until every drop of blood drawn with the lash shall be paid by another drawn with the sword, as was said three thousand years ago, so still it must be said, "The judgments of the Lord are true and righteous altogether."

With malice toward none, with charity for all, with firmness in the right as God gives us to see the right, let us strive on to finish the work we are in, to bind up the nation's wounds, to care for him who shall have borne the battle and for his widow and his orphan, to do all which may achieve and cherish a just and lasting peace among ourselves and with all nations.

JOHN F. KENNEDY

Inaugural Address

John Fitzgerald Kennedy (1917–1963) was born in Brookline, Massachusetts, won his B.A. from Harvard in 1940 and published *Why England Slept* the same year. He was in the United States Navy from 1941 to 1945, became a Congressman from Massachusetts in 1947 and Senator in 1953, and defeated Richard Nixon for the Presidency by a narrow margin in 1960. He was assassinated in Dallas, Texas, on November 22, 1963.

Vice President Johnson, Mr. Speaker, Mr. Chief Justice, President Eisenhower, Vice President Nixon, President Truman, Reverend Clergy, fellow citizens: *

We observe today not a victory of party but a celebration of freedom — symbolizing an end as well as a beginning — signifying renewal as well as change. For I have sworn before you and Almighty God the same solemn oath our forebears prescribed nearly a century and three-quarters ago.

The world is very different now. For man holds in his mortal hands the power to abolish all forms of human poverty and all forms of human life. And yet the same revolutionary beliefs for which our forebears fought are still at issue around the globe — the belief that the rights of man come not from the generosity of the state but from the hand of God.

We dare not forget today that we are the heirs of that first revolution. Let the word go forth from this time and place, to friend and foe alike, that the torch has been passed to a new generation of Americans — born in this century, tempered by war, disciplined by a hard and bitter peace, proud of our ancient heritage — and unwilling to witness or permit the slow undoing of those human rights to which this nation has always been committed, and to which we are committed today at home and around the world.

Let every nation know, whether it wishes us well or ill, that we shall pay any price, bear any burden, meet any hardship, support any friend, oppose any foe to assure the survival and the success of liberty.

This much we pledge — and more.

* From *Public Papers of the Presidents — John F. Kennedy, 1961.* (Washington, 1962) pp. 1–3.

To those old allies whose cultural and spiritual origins we share, we pledge the loyalty of faithful friends. United, there is little we cannot do in a host of cooperative ventures. Divided, there is little we can do — for we dare not meet a powerful challenge at odds and split asunder.

To those new states whom we welcome to the ranks of the free, we pledge our word that one form of colonial control shall not have passed away merely to be replaced by a far more iron tyranny. We shall not always expect to find them supporting our view. But we shall always hope to find them strongly supporting their own freedom — and to remember that, in the past, those who foolishly sought power by riding the back of the tiger ended up inside.

To those peoples in the huts and villages of half the globe struggling to break the bonds of mass misery, we pledge our best efforts to help them help themselves, for whatever period is required — not because the communists may be doing it, not because we seek their votes, but because it is right. If a free society cannot help the many who are poor, it cannot save the few who are rich.

To our sister republics south of our border, we offer a special pledge — to convert our good words into good deeds — in a new alliance for progress — to assist free men and free governments in casting off the chains of poverty. But this peaceful revolution of hope cannot become the prey of hostile powers. Let all our neighbors know that we shall join with them to oppose aggression or subversion anywhere in the Americas. And let every other power know that this Hemisphere intends to remain the master of its own house.

To that world assembly of sovereign states, the United Nations, our last best hope in an age where the instruments of war have far outpaced the instruments of peace, we renew our pledge of support — to prevent it from becoming merely a forum for invective — to strengthen its shield of the new and the weak — and to enlarge the area in which its writ may run.

Finally, to those nations who would make themselves our adversary, we offer not a pledge but a request: that both sides begin anew the quest for peace, before the dark powers of destruction unleashed by science engulf all humanity in planned or accidental self-destruction.

We dare not tempt them with weakness. For only when our arms are sufficient beyond doubt can we be certain beyond doubt that they will never be employed.

But neither can two great and powerful groups of nations take comfort from our present course — both sides overburdened by the cost of modern weapons, both rightly alarmed by the steady spread of the deadly atom, yet both racing to alter that uncertain balance of terror that stays the hand of mankind's final war.

So let us begin anew — remembering on both sides that civility is not a sign of weakness, and sincerity is always subject to proof. Let us never negotiate out of fear. But let us never fear to negotiate.

Let both sides explore what problems unite us instead of belaboring those problems which divide us.

Let both sides, for the first time, formulate serious and precise proposals for the inspection and control of arms — and bring the absolute power to destroy other nations under the absolute control of all nations.

Let both sides seek to invoke the wonders of science instead of its terrors. Together let us explore the stars, conquer the deserts, eradicate disease, tap the ocean depths and encourage the arts and commerce.

Let both sides unite to heed in all corners of the earth the command of Isaiah — to "undo the heavy burdens . . . [and] let the oppressed go free."

And if a beachhead of cooperation may push back the jungles of suspicion, let both sides join in creating a new endeavor — not a new balance of power, but a new world of law, where the strong are just and the weak secure and the peace preserved.

All this will not be finished in the first one hundred days. Nor will it be finished in the first one thousand days, nor in the life of this Administration, nor even perhaps in our lifetime on this planet. But let us begin.

In your hands, my fellow citizens, more than mine, will rest the final success or failure of our course. Since this country was founded, each generation of Americans has been summoned to give testimony to its national loyalty. The graves of young Americans who answered the call to service surround the globe.

Now the trumpet summons us again — not as a call to bear arms, though arms we need — not as a call to battle, though embattled we are — but a call to bear the burden of a long twilight struggle, year in and year out, "rejoicing in hope, patient in tribulation" — a struggle against the common enemies of man: tyranny, poverty, disease and war itself.

Can we forge against these enemies a grand and global alliance, North and South, East and West, that can assure a more fruitful life for all mankind? Will you join in that historic effort?

In the long history of the world, only a few generations have been granted the role of defending freedom in its hour of maximum danger. I do not shrink from this responsibility — I welcome it. I do not believe that any of us would exchange places with any other people or any other generation. The energy, the faith, the devotion which we bring to this endeavor will light our country and all who serve it — and the glow from that fire can truly light the world.

And so, my fellow Americans: ask not what your country can do for you — ask what you can do for your country.

My fellow citizens of the world: ask not what America will do for you, but what together we can do for the freedom of man.

Finally, whether you are citizens of America or citizens of the world, ask of us here the same high standards of strength and sacrifice which we ask of you. With a good conscience our only sure reward, with history the final judge of our deeds, let us go forth to lead the land we love, asking His blessing and His help, but knowing that here on earth God's work must truly be our own.

VIII
Journalists at Work and Play

Politics has given steadier employment to many journalists than to some politicians, and some political columnists have undoubtedly influenced thinking in governmental circles if not indeed the curve of events. For the run-of-the-mill column the daily paper provides examples at every level of quality. For our purposes we have chosen samples from the political writer, James B. Reston, and the occasionally political columnist, Art Buchwald.

JAMES RESTON

Uniquack Explains de Gaulle

Here James B. Reston utilizes his invention, Uniquack, to solve the mystery of General de Gaulle. The time was early February, 1963.* In the previous month the French President had vetoed Britain's admission to the Common Market and rejected an American proposal for a NATO nuclear force. Mr. Reston, the political commentator, was born in Scotland in 1909, brought to the United States in 1910, graduated from the University of Illinois in 1932. Since 1953 he has been chief Washington correspondent of *The New York Times*.

Washington, Feb. 2. A perplexed lady in California wants to know what Uniquack thinks about the present state of the world, and since we have nothing else to do today, we got the thing out and put some questions to it.

Uniquack, for the benefit of any newcomers, is an electronic truth-detector which, when seated in a comfortable room by a glowing fire

* From *The New York Times*, Western edition, Feb. 4, 1963, p. 6 with the kind permission of James Reston and *The New York Times*. © 1963 by *The New York Times* Company.

and supplied with sufficient quantities of alcohol, can translate and de-contaminate official documents and even understand politicians.

Question: All right, machine, let's start with an easy one. Please explain General de Gaulle.

Answer: Certainly. General de Gaulle, like vintage wine and Brigitte Bardot, is one of the great natural resources of France. He is a symbol of his country's regret and glory. He is unique among the statesmen of the Western world because (a) he knows what he wants, (b) speaks sparingly and eloquently, (c) doesn't give a damn for popularity, and (d) uses the word "no." He's sort of the opposite of that insular, seafaring type Mr. Micawber: He's always looking for something to turn down.

Q: Please don't be frivolous today, machine. The lady in California wants serious answers about the fight between Kennedy and de Gaulle.

A: Well, the difference between them comes down to this: Kennedy thinks the cold war is still serious, and de Gaulle thinks Kennedy has won it and doesn't know it. Kennedy thinks the problem in Europe is military and de Gaulle thinks it's political. The General is not worried about Russian soldiers taking over Europe but about British statesmen and American salesmen, generals and politicians taking it over.

Q: I see. Co-colonialism is the enemy.

A: Precisely. He sees time and history in another way. He tunes in the world on his private wave-length. He cannot forgive the Anglo-Saxons for the favors they have done him. Having lost an empire with the help of an army, he is determined to gain a continent without one.

Q: You mean he just doesn't like us?

A: No, it isn't that. He just doesn't want to marry us. Actually, in his own way he is paying us a tribute. He thinks we have saved Europe and split the Communist world, and he doesn't trust his own people to stand up to our barbarian ways.

Q: So he would have us go away.

A: No, he merely wants American protection without domination, and no incineration without representation. What's wrong with that?

Q: He wants to have it both ways.

A: Certainly, and he'll get it because we can't hurt him without hurting Europe and ourselves. He thinks the centuries balance the books: in the 19th, America united and developed behind the sea power of Europe; in the 20th, Europe will unite and develop behind the rocket power of America. It's all very simple.

Q: You are beginning to sound slightly Gaullist and subversive, machine. I suppose de Gaulle thinks he will unite Europe.

A: No, not precisely. He believes Europe will be united, not by de Gaulle, or Macmillan, Kennedy or Khrushchev, but by Mao Tse-tung. He thinks the Chinese Communists will scare some sense into the Russians, and that the Russians will eventually come to terms with de Gaulle and Western Europe.

Q: It's all very tidy, isn't it? But when is "eventually" and how will the Germans like this French Rapallo? [1]

A: "Eventually" in de Gaulle's mind is sooner than you think. He has already made a trade agreement with Moscow this weekend and even if the Germans don't like it, only Russia can put the two Germanys together.

Q: I see that Joseph Alsop thinks de Gaulle will outlast Kennedy in office. What do you think of that?

A: I don't know about Mr. Alsop's sources of information on these matters, but I doubt it. God is said to be jealous, as you know, and since de Gaulle has recently been muscling in on His business, God could get bored with him.

Q: What about Khrushchev's role in all this?

A: A very cunning and devious man. He has deceived the West. In the past, when the Western allies began quarreling with each other he has always made some violent lurch that has brought them back together. We have come to count on this. Fear is our ally, we need his hostility more now than ever, but he has doublecrossed us. He is now talking peace and trade and sending messages of condolence on the death of Robert Frost. It is a very serious situation.

Q: And the British?

A: They will never forgive de Gaulle. An Englishman can stand anything except being rejected by a club — especially when he thinks he's too good for it anyway.[2]

Q: And finally, what should Washington do?

A: Shut up. Tight.

Q: An original idea, but how?

A: Any official who makes a speech, holds a press conference, peddles a Polaris submarine, mentions the words de Gaulle, Napoleon or Joan of Arc, or talks even privately about Canada for at least a month should be fired.

Q: And meanwhile?

A: Let them think.

Q: Really, machine, you have the most preposterous ideas.

[1] This refers to a Russo-German treaty of friendship and commerce concluded at Rapallo in 1922.
[2] Britain declined to join the Common Market when it was founded, was turned down when she applied.

ART BUCHWALD

Congressional Featherbedding

In the summer of 1963, political observers began predicting that the dragging tempo of the 88th Congress (1st Session) would make it invidiously unique. The following satire by Art Buchwald had the distinction of being read into the *Congressional Record* on successive days by Senators who strongly advocated the modernization of Congress: the late Estes Kefauver of Tennessee and Joseph Clark of Pennsylvania.* Mr. Buchwald was born in Mount Vernon, N. Y., in 1925, attended the University of Southern California, has been a columnist since 1948, and has written several books.

Destructionalism Art Created in Abstract

Many people are wondering how Congress can remain in session for as long as it has without passing any important legislation. Well, it isn't easy. It takes experience, knowhow, and devoted patience.

The Members of the 88th Congress have the art of legislative featherbedding down to a science, and after spending time on Capitol Hill one can't help developing anything but admiration for our elected representatives. To paraphrase Sir Winston Churchill, "Never have so few done so little for so many."

How do they do it? In order to find out, we interviewed a Congressman who was willing to talk providing we didn't use his name.

"Sir, how are you able to stay in session for so long without doing anything?"

"The secret is cooperation, boy," he said. "Without cooperation from everybody in Congress, Heaven knows how many laws we'd pass."

"What do you mean, sir?"

"Well, boy, Congress has built-in safeguards against anything getting on the floor for a vote. For one thing, a bill has to go to a committee for study. The bill is usually given to the committee that is most unfavorable to its being passed, so it's pigeon-holed without much discussion. In most cases the key committees in Congress are controlled by chairmen who are pledged to keeping legislation away from the legislators."

"Why is that?"

"If you, as a legislator, vote, that means you're taking a stand on an issue, and if you're running for reelection the last thing you want to do is to let the voters know what side you're on."

* *Congressional Record,* Vol. 109, p. A4983 (Aug. 6) and pp. 13630–31 (Aug. 7). Reprinted with the kind permission of Art Buchwald and the *New York Herald Tribune.*

"Then as a safeguard we also have the congressional hearing. You can have hearings for as long as nine months on a piece of legislation. Sometimes, if the legislation is newsworthy enough, you can have two or three committees holding hearings on the same bill at the same time. In many cases the hearings become so complicated the committee forgets why they're holding them in the first place. But as long as the hearings get in the newspapers everyone is satisfied."

"Who decides whether a hearing has enough publicity value?"

"Usually the chairman of the committee. We depend on him to hold hearings only on legislation that will get our names in the papers."

"But there have been occasions where a bill has gotten to the floor of the House. How do you explain that?"

"Somebody goofed. He is usually censured in private for it, and we see that he doesn't get to handle any bills again. But fortunately, even if a bill gets to the floor, we have safeguards against passing it. For one thing, you need a quorum and it isn't easy to get one.

"Most Congressmen go home on Thursdays and come back on Tuesdays. Then they have mail to answer, speaking engagements to fulfill, and interviews to give to the press. Very few Congressmen have time to vote."

"But suppose you do have a quorum and you do vote and you do pass a bill. Then what?"

"It's happened in previous Congresses," he admitted. "But very rarely in ours. If this did happen, we would then depend on the Senate not to pass it. That's why we have two Houses. So each one has a chance to cancel out the other's bill. We're pledged to kill their bills and they're pledged to kill ours."

IX / A Plea for Peace

Since the advent of the Atomic Age prospects for peace have been anxiously surveyed on radio and television, in the pulpit and press, in periodicals and in books. Included here as our final document is a remarkable essay by Norman Cousins. Other important and eloquent statements on this subject are former President Eisenhower's dramatic "Atoms for Peace" proposals laid before the General Assembly of the United Nations in December, 1953; U. N. Secretary-General U Thant's address before the American Association for the United Nations, November 17, 1962; the late President Kennedy's speech, "The Strategy of Peace," at American University, June 10, 1963; and the late Pope John XXIII's encyclical, "Peace on Earth," of April 10, 1963.

NORMAN COUSINS

Modern Man Is Obsolete

Less than two weeks after the Atomic Age made its shattering entrance at Hiroshima, this dramatic and imperative essay appeared as an editorial in *The Saturday Review of Literature.** Its author, Norman Cousins, was born at Union Hill, N. J., in 1912, studied at Columbia, became editor of *The Saturday Review* in 1942.

Whatever elation there is in the world today because of final victory in the war is severely tempered by fear. It is a primitive fear, the fear of the unknown, the fear of forces man can neither channel nor comprehend. This fear is not new; in its classical form it is the fear of irrational death. But overnight it has become intensified, magnified. It has burst out of the subconscious and into the conscious, filling the mind with primordial apprehensions. It is thus that man stumbles fitfully into

* From *The Saturday Review of Literature,* vol. 28, Pt. 2, Aug. 18, 1945, pp. 5–9. Reprinted by permission of Norman Cousins.

a new age of atomic energy for which he is as ill equipped to accept its potential blessings as he is to counteract or control its present dangers.

Where man can find no answer, he will find fear. While the dust was still settling over Hiroshima, he was asking himself questions and finding no answers. The biggest question of these concerns the nature of man. Is war in the nature of man? If so, how much time has he left before he employs the means he has already devised for the ultimate in self-destruction — extinction? And now that the science of warfare has reached the point where it threatens the planet itself, is it possible that man is destined to return the earth to its aboriginal incandescent mass blazing at fifty million degrees? If not — that is, if war is not in the nature of man — then how is he to interpret his own experience, which tells him that in all of recorded history there have been only 300 years in the aggregate during which he has been free of war?

Closely following upon these are other questions, flowing out endlessly from his fears and without prospect of definitive answer. Even assuming that he could hold destructive science in check, what changes would the new age bring or demand in his everyday life? What changes would it bring or demand in his culture, his education, his philosophy, his religion, his relationships with other human beings?

In speculating upon these questions, it should not be necessary to prove that on August 6, 1945, a new age was born. When on that day a parachute containing a small object floated to earth over Japan, it marked the violent death of one stage in man's history and the beginning of another. Nor should it be necessary to prove the saturating effect of the new age, permeating every aspect of man's activities, from machines to morals, from physics to philosophy, from politics to poetry; in sum, it is an effect creating a blanket of obsolescence not only over the methods and the products of man but over man himself.

It is a curious phenomenon of nature that only two species practise the art of war — men and ants, both of which, ironically, maintain complex social organizations. . . . It is encouraging to note that while all entomologists are agreed that war is instinctive with ants, not all anthropologists and biologists are agreed that war is instinctive with men. The strict empiricists, of course, find everything in man's history to indicate that war is locked up with his nature. But a broader and more generous, certainly more philosophical, view is held by those scientists who claim that the evidence to date is incomplete and misleading and that man *does* have within him the power of abolishing war. . . .

But even if this gives us a reassuring answer to the question — is war inevitable because of man's nature? — it still leaves unanswered the question concerning the causes leading up to war. The expression of man's nature will continue to be warlike if the same conditions are continued that have provoked warlike expressions in him in the past. And since man's survival on earth is now absolutely dependent on his ability to avoid a new war, he is faced with the so-far insoluble problem of eliminating those causes.

In the most primitive sense, war in man is an expression of his competitive impulses. Like everything else in nature, he has had to fight for existence; but the battle against other animals, once won, gave way in his evolution to battle against his own kind. Darwin called it the survival of the fittest, and its most over-stretched interpretation is to be found in "Mein Kampf," with its naked glorification of brute force and the complete worship of might makes right. In the political and national sense, it has been the attempt of the "have-nots" to take from the "haves," or the attempt of the "haves" to add further to their lot at the expense of the "have-nots." Not always was property at stake; comparative advantages were measured in terms of power, and in terms of tribal or national superiority. The good luck of one nation became the hard luck of another. The good fortune of the Western powers in obtaining "concessions" in China at the turn of the century was the ill fortune of the Chinese. The power that Germany stripped from Austria, Czechoslovakia, Poland and France at the beginning of World War II she added to her own.

What does it matter, then, if war is not in the nature of man so long as man continues through the expression of his nature to be a viciously competitive animal? The effect is the same, and therefore the result must be as conclusive — war being the effect, and complete obliteration of the human species being the result.

If this reasoning is correct, then modern man is obsolete, a self-made anachronism becoming more incongruous by the minute. He has exalted change in everything but himself. He has leaped centuries ahead in inventing a new world to live in, but he knows little or nothing about his own part in that world. He has surrounded and confounded himself with gaps — gaps between revolutionary science and evolutionary anthropology, between cosmic gadgets and human wisdom, between intellect and conscience. The struggle between science and morals that Henry Thomas Buckle foresaw a century ago has been all but won. by science. Given time, man might be expected to bridge those gaps normally; but by his own hand, he is destroying even time. Communication, transportation, war no longer wait on time. Decision and execution in the modern world are becoming virtually synchronous. Thus, whatever bridges man has to build and cross he shall have to build and cross immediately.

This involves both biology and will. If he lacks the actual and potential biological equipment to build those bridges, then the birth certificate of the atomic age is in reality a *memento mori*. But even if he possesses the necessary biological equipment, he must still make the decision which says that he is to apply himself to the challenge. Capability without decision is inaction and inconsequence.

Man is left then with a crisis in decision. The main test before him involves his will to change rather than his ability to change. . . . That is why the quintessence of destruction as potentially represented by modern science must be dramatized and kept in the forefront of public opinion. The full dimensions of the peril must be seen and recognized. Then and only then will man realize that the first order of business is the question of continued existence. Then and only then will he be prepared to make the decisions necessary to assure that survival.

In making these decisions, there are two principal courses that are open to him. Both will keep him alive for an indefinite or at least a reasonably long period. These courses, however, are directly contradictory and represent polar extremes of approach.

The first course is the positive approach. It begins with a careful survey and appraisal of the obsolescences which constitute the afterbirth of the new age. The survey must begin with man himself. . . . No amount of tinkering with his institutions will be sufficient to insure his survival unless he can make the necessary adjustments in his own relationship to the world and to society.

The first adjustment or mutation needed in the expression of his nature . . . is his savagely competitive impulses. In the pre-Atomic Age, those impulses were natural and occasionally justifiable, though they often led to war. . . . [The] dominant feature [of that Age] was an insufficiency of the goods and the needs of life. . . .

Yet all this has been — or can be — changed by the new age. Man now has it within his grasp to emancipate himself economically. If he wills it, he is in a position to refine his competitive impulse; he can take the step from competitive man to cooperative man. He has at last unlocked enough of the earth's secrets to provide for his needs on a world scale. . . .

It is here that man's survey of himself needs the severest scrutiny, for he is his own greatest obstacle to the achievement of those attainable and necessary goals. . . . He has shattered the atom and harnessed its fabulous power to a bomb, but he balks — or allows himself to be balked — when it comes to harnessing that power for human progress. Already, many representatives of industry have counseled words of synthetic caution, informing a puzzled public that we shall not see the practical application of atomic energy for general use in our lifetime. . . .

This is not a matter of urging a change away from the present economic structure just for the sake of change; it is recognition of a hard new fact of life that has made that economic structure obsolete in an Atomic Age just as it has made practically all our other institutions obsolete. . . .

The size of the opportunity is exceeded only by the size of the promise. But even as man stands on the threshold of a new age, he is being pulled back by his coattails and told to look the other way, told that he must not allow his imagination to get out of hand — all this at a time when he should know almost instinctively that if he can put the same courage, daring, imagination, ingenuity, and skill that he demonstrated in winning the war into meeting the problems of the new age, he can win the peace as well.

He must believe, too, that mobilization of science and knowledge in peace should not be confined to cosmic forces, but must be extended to his other needs, principally health. What a fantastic irony that organized science knows the secret of the atom but as yet knows not a fig about the common cold! . . .

Surveying other adjustments he shall have to make if he chooses the positive course, man must consider himself in relation to his individual development. He can have the limitless opportunities that can come with time to think. The trend during the last fifty years towards shorter work weeks and shorter hours will not only be continued but sharply accelerated. . . . But a revolution is needed in his leisure-time activities. . . . He shall have to effect a radical transformation in his approach to and philosophy of education, which must prepare him for the opportunities and responsibilities not only of his chosen work but for the business of living itself. The primary aim should be the development of a critical intelligence. The futile war now going on between specialization and general study must be stopped. There need no longer be any conflict between the two. The individual will need both. . . . As for the problem of time in which to accomplish these dual objectives, formalized education until the twenty-fifth or thirtieth year is doubtless indicated. . . .

We have saved for last the most crucial aspect of this general survey relating to the first course: the transformation or adjustment from national man to world man. Already he has become a world warrior; it is but one additional step — though a long one — for him to develop a world conscience. This is not vaporous idealism, but sheer driving necessity. It bears directly on the prospects of his own survival. He shall have to recognize the flat truth that the greatest obsolescence of all in the Atomic Age is national sovereignty. Even back in the old-fashioned rocket age before August 6, 1945, strict national sovereignty was an anomalous and preposterous hold-over from the tribal instinct in nations. If it was anomalous then, it is the quintessence of anomaly now. . . .

Reject all other arguments for *real* world government . . . valid though they may be. Consider only the towering problem of policing the atom — the problem of keeping the smallest particle of matter from destroying all matter. We are building on soapbubbles if we expect this problem to be automatically solved by having America, Britain and Canada keep the secret to themselves. . . . In all history, there is not a single instance of a new weapon being kept exclusively by any power or powers. . . .

Nor can we rely on destructive atomic energy to take care of itself. Already there is the tempting but dangerous notion to the effect that the atomic bomb is so horrible and the terror of retaliation so great that we may have seen the last of war. . . . If history teaches us anything, it is that the possibility of war increases in direct proportion to the effectiveness of the instruments of war.

Far from banishing war, the atomic bomb will in itself constitute a cause of war. In the absence of world control as part of world government, it will create universal fear and suspicion. Each nation will live nervously from one moment to the next, not knowing whether the designs or ambitions of other nations might prompt them to attempt a lightning blow of obliteration. . . .

No; there is no comfort to be derived from the war-is-now-too-horrible theory. There is one way and only one to achieve effective control of destructive atomic energy and that is through centralized world government. Not loose, informal organization. . . . The potency of the weapon must dictate the potency of its control. . . .

It would be comforting to know that the world has several generations in which it might be able to evolve naturally and progressively into a single governmental unit. . . . But the time factor has been shattered. We no longer have a leeway of fifteen or twenty years; whatever must be done must be done with an immediacy which is in keeping with the urgency. . . .

If all this sounds like headlong argument, posing methods or solutions which seem above the reach of mortal man, the answer must be that mortal man's reach was long enough apparently to push science and invention ahead by at least five hundred years during five years of experimentation on atomic energy. His ability to do this not only indicates that he can extend or over-extend himself when pressed, but emphasizes the need to do the same with government.

In meeting this need, man need not be frightened by the enormity of the differences which shall have to be accommodated within the world structure. . . . The important question is not how great an obstacle the differences may be to the setting up of a closely knit world structure, but whether man will be in a better position to reconcile those differences within world government than without it.

Man must decide, moreover, what is more important — his differences or his similarities. If he chooses the former, he embarks on a path that will, paradoxically, destroy the differences and himself as well. . . .

True, in making the jump to world government, man is taking a big chance. Not only does he have to create the first world authority, but he shall have to make sure that this authority is wisely used. The world institution must be compatible with — indeed, must promote — free institutions. . . . We have too often allowed the best ideas to fall into the hands of the worst men. . . . It was in the name of socialism and social progress that Fascism came to Italy and Nazism to Germany.

That is the double nature of the challenge: to bring about world government and keep it pure. It is a large order, perhaps the largest order man has had to meet in his 50,000 years on earth, but he himself has set up the conditions which have made the order necessary.

All these are the various mutations and adjustments needed in the expression of man's nature, in his way of life, his thinking, his economics, his education, his conditioning and orientation, and his concept of government in an Atomic Age. But if he rejects this, the first course, there is yet another way, an alternative to world government. This is the second course. Preposterous as this second course may seem, we describe it in all seriousness, for it is possible that through it man may find a way to stay alive — which is the central problem under consideration in this paper.

The second course is relatively simple. It requires that man destroy, carefully and completely, everything relating to science and civilization. Let him destroy all machines and the knowledge which can build or operate those machines. Let him raze his cities, smash his laboratories, dismantle his factories, tear down his universities and schools, burn his libraries, rip apart his art. Let him murder his scientists, his doctors, his teachers, his lawmakers, his mechanics, his merchants, and anyone who has anything to do with the machinery of knowledge or progress. Let him punish literacy by death. Let him abolish nations and set up the tribe as sovereign. In short, let him revert to his condition in society in 10,000 B.C. Thus emancipated from science, from progress, from government, from knowledge, from thought, he can be reasonably certain of safeguarding his existence on this planet.

This is the alternative to world government — if modern man wishes an alternative.

Study Aids

ORWELL: Prose and Politics

1. In this essay Orwell argues that language is "an instrument which we [can] shape for our own purposes," and that improvement in speech and writing should result in better political practices. Before you accept his persuasive argument you will want to challenge it. Is it possible to *dictate* language habits? How do such habits arise? How successful have Ireland and Israel been in imposing a language? What comes first, the political act, or the language on which it depends? If political writing is largely the defense of the indefensible, as Orwell insists, would not the politician find vague verbiage more effective to his purposes than the direct, honest prose here advocated?

2. Has this essay affected your awareness of values in the use of words, or persuaded you to examine and perhaps improve your own writing and speech? If so, how did Orwell accomplish his purpose? Was it facts, argument, organization, ridicule, choice of words and phrases, or what?

3. Orwell lists several swindles or tricks, such as dying metaphors, pretentious diction, etc. Later he says he has certainly committed some of the faults he lists. Can you find examples; or better, point out metaphors which are alive, words and phrases which are at once simple and expressive, etc.?

4. Do you agree with Orwell's downgrading of foreign words? Is this an example of English chauvinism (to use a bad foreign word)? Wouldn't the single word *cliché* have saved him a phrase here and there, and been quite as direct and exact?

5. Orwell once confessed that he had a horror of politics, which he charges here with deceit, brutality, murder. Is his characterization of politics fair or accurate? If it is, can we expect to improve politics simply by choosing better words?

6. Can you match Orwell's samples of English to be avoided by scavenging in the newspapers and magazines?

MACHIAVELLI: Principles and Politics

1. Can you state Michiavelli's central thought in a single sentence?

2. One of Machiavelli's aims was to free Lorenzo de' Medici from scruples that might limit his success. What means does he employ to quiet the prince's conscience? How does he suggest that the Church would not object to princely fraud? Does he appeal to the prince's reason, his self-esteem, his ambition, his honor?

3. Throughout the essay there are pairs (man and beast) and dualism (good courses and evil courses). Unexpectedly the prince is not asked to choose *one,* but *both.* Is it humanly possible to be both good and evil? How does Machiavelli resolve the contradiction? Is his advice meant for all men, or for princes only?

4. Machiavelli expresses a low opinion of mankind, but advises the prince to play the hypocrite to win public esteem. What is his purpose in doing so?

5. The lion and the fox have had symbolic meaning from ancient times. Do they serve any useful purpose in this essay?

6. How would you rate the following on a Machiavellian scale: Franklin D. Roosevelt, General de Gaulle, Churchill, Hitler, Mussolini, Stalin, Chiang Kai-shek? Do you find any correlation between principle and success in their careers?

LASSWELL: Symbols in Political Manipulation

1. Mr. Lasswell says that symbols "of the common destiny" are the "ideology" of the existing order, "the utopia" of the counter-elites. If this means that revolutionaries use the symbols and slogans of the regimes they seek to destroy, to what degree was it true of the French or Russian Revolutions or of the Nazi movement? Is it true of extremists on right and left in the United States today? Does it harmonize with his paragraph beginning "The object of revolution"? Do your answers require any rephrasing of Mr. Lasswell's statement above?

2. Mr. Lasswell states that the object of revolution is to "attain coercive predominance over the enemy as a means of working one's will with him." Can you think of a better way to say it?

3. Here society is divided into an elite and "the masses" out of which counter-elites may emerge. Does Mr. Lasswell say anything that suggests where his own sympathies lie? Would anything he says be helpful to an elite or to its opponents in planning a course of action, whether defensive or revolutionary?

4. Is he cynical or merely objective about our conditioning from cradle to grave? Are the details of his "precious haze" of childhood in any degree dated?

5. Does he imply that a Fascist movement would be more likely to suc-

ceed in the United States than a revolutionary movement? Would he say the same thing today?

6. Could you rephrase the final sentence to communicate whatever meaning it has? Does the writer mean that propaganda employing symbols may fail to incite if the time is not right?

BROGAN: America Is Words

1. Would you describe "America Is Words" as closely knit, informal, learned, genial, rambling, entertaining, consistent, verbose, assertive, authoritative? How would you defend your judgment?

2. Mr. Brogan writes confidently about the American audience, and about various American traits. What is the basis of his generalizations? Observation? Conversation? Reading? Does he suggest the possibility of regional differences, or of changes over time? He wrote this book during World War II. Do any of his observations or topical allusions strike you as out of date? Which ones, and why?

3. Does Mr. Brogan write about us as friend, foe or neutral? What are the least flattering things he says about us? Do you detect any tendency to follow a hard critical remark by a pleasant or obscure softener? When he noted a difference between us and the British, why did he say they, not we, were out of step? How would you rephrase his critical comments to indicate hostility?

4. Is there any inconsistency in his noting our skepticism at one point and our gullibility at another? Do you agree that we have no fear of eloquence, clichés, bathos uttered by our politicians? If so does this mean that we are generally uncritical, or merely that we believe the politician's role requires him to shun most of Mr. Orwell's excellent advice?

WEBSTER: Liberty and Union

1. A later Senator from Massachusetts, Henry Cabot Lodge, once described Webster as "Attic" in subordinating form to thought in contrast to the florid style of "the so-called Asiatics." Do you agree that Webster's thought is not obscured or interrupted by verbal flourishes? How would you characterize his style? What changes of tone occur in the passages we have quoted here?

2. Once Webster calls the doctrine of nullification an absurdity. How much does his argument depend on name-calling or ridicule?

3. What would Webster have answered if asked when and where the people ever "declared that this Constitution shall be the supreme law?"

4. Webster's eloquence has been said to overpower and oppress as well as convince. Are these traits apparent here?

5. By what argument does Webster provide justification for the South's later secession?

6. Why did Webster introduce the interlude on treason and hanging? Is the

grim humor meant to dissuade the South, or merely to relieve tension, as Shakespeare's horseplay often did? Could he be trying to promote a difference of opinion in South Carolina between the honest militiamen and the top brass?

7. In the eloquent peroration how does Webster direct his appeal to reason as well as to emotion?

BROOKS: Webster the Man

1. Would you say that Mr. Brooks' description of Webster is deliberately unrestrained or intemperate? Is his style or tone meant to suggest something of Webster's? Does Mr. Brooks sound a little demiurgic in his very long second sentence? Can you find its subject and predicate?

2. Mark the words and phrases that contribute to the impression of Webster as a hero of special quality and stature.

3. How much of this sketch is to be taken as the legendary Webster? Is there any way of knowing whether Mr. Brooks added a few purely fictive bits? If the legend begins in paragraph two, does it end with the vertical burial of Webster's horses?

4. What was it in Webster, his views or his habits, that endeared him to different classes in Massachusetts society? Would anyone have disapproved of Webster's "ample faults?"

5. How do you explain Webster being "almost a foreigner" in the first paragraph and the archetype American in the last?

6. What is the meaning of "as a lawyer, he [Webster] was unapproachable"? We know that he practised law while a member of Congress, and well-to-do clients had no difficulty in approaching him.

BEVERIDGE: The Philippines Are Ours Forever

1. The phrase "territory belonging to the United States" occurs in Article IV, Section 3 of the Constitution. To what does it refer? Does it provide an adequate constitutional base for a colonial empire?

2. In paragraph two, Senator Beveridge uses a series of parallel sentences ("We will not repudiate . . ." "We will not abandon . . ." "We will not renounce . . ."). This rhetorical device suggests that corresponding parts of the sentences are similar in meaning and value and that if you accept one you should accept the others. But note that between *duty* and *mission* comes *opportunity* which refers back to China's great markets. Near the end also America's *interests* are almost concealed among references to *God, saving forces, glory* and *duty*. To what extent is this alternation of moral purpose and commercialism an effective appeal to Beveridge's audience?

3. How does the orator's use of short, blunt sentences contribute to the impression of "candor" he wishes to convey?

4. What moral or even theological assumptions are contained in the statement that God has not been preparing us for "nothing but vain and idle self-

contemplation and self-admiration?" What Senator could have risked replying that He has?

5. Note how many strikes the orator's opponents had against them: they were unmindful of duty, gain, or the will of God; they were sluggard, blind, craven, etc. If you had to answer Senator Beveridge, what could you have said if you had agreed with him, or if you had disagreed? In fact Senator Hoar of Massachusetts spoke next, and he began by referring contemptuously to Beveridge's "glittering temple of glass," and said he had missed any reference to Right, Justice, or Freedom in all his eloquence. (Philippine independence was voted by Congress in 1934 to take effect in 1946; it hadn't a chance in 1900.)

6. How might an African student of today respond to Senator Beveridge's view that most races are destined to indefinite tutelage?

7. What did World War II do to the notion that the Philippines were the Gibraltar of the Pacific and the key to its domination?

DUNNE: Mr. Dooley on Taking the Philippines

1. Satire may be directed at folly and employ irony, ridicule, etc. Is the satire here directed toward the public's role in empire-building, or toward more general problems of a democracy? Do you find any irony or ridicule?

2. The public is expected to form opinions on important questions. Could opinions based on the false and contradictory information suggested here have any validity? Does Dunne blame anyone?

3. In the dialogue what is Mr. Hennessy's function? How does he differ from Mr. Dooley? Is Mr. Dooley merely an uncultured bartender? Is he ever consciously ironic? Does he really expect to wake up some morning with the right answer, as President McKinley admitted to doing?

4. Why does Dunne name Mr. Dooley's competitor Schwartzmeister?

5. What happens when you translate a few sentences of Mr. Dooley's discourse into your own prose? Do you have to modify the thought to give it credibility? What happens to the fantasy of Mr. Dooley tossing bombs into Havana from behind his own bar?

6. When urged "to take in" the Filipinos and to clothe them, Mr. Dooley said he had no bed to spare and but a suit to his name. Is the author ridiculing anyone who looks on his nation's commitments as his own? Or is this a way of contrasting a citizen who takes empire-building seriously and responsibly with the light-hearted flag-wavers who would share the benefits but not the burdens?

SMITH: Free Trade Is Nature's Way

1. Much of Adam Smith's argument now sounds commonplace, but his thesis was revolutionary in 1776. What means does he employ for minimizing the alarm, fears, or indignation of his readers?

2. How does he establish his law that one's pursuit of private gain is "necessarily" most advantageous to society? Do you agree? Can you think of exceptions that Smith himself would have to allow?

3. Here he argues for free trade by comparing a family with the kingdom. Is there a flaw in the analogy?

4. In his discussion of retaliatory tariffs, he departs from his customary bland tone to call the politician an "insidious and crafty animal." Is this unpleasant characterization intended to throw light on the point at issue, or to contribute to his general theme that economic affairs prosper more as politicians interfere less?

5. Near the end Smith calmly concedes that freedom of trade is not likely to be entirely "restored" in Britain, but then raises his voice against the monopolists who intimidate government and threaten honest men with violence. The virtual tirade suddenly ends and the tone becomes again cool and reasonable. Was the author merely expressing emotion, or was he employing a tactic of persuasion?

TAWNEY: Freedom and Economic Inequality

1. What is Mr. Tawney's theme? Is he more interested in saying what the evil is than in prescribing for its cure? In what degree is he teacher, philosopher, preacher, propagandist, agitator?

2. To what audience would his style of writing and his argument appeal? A critic in 1931 wrote that Mr. Tawney was master of a classical style which "was the more effective because out of fashion." Do you agree?

3. Does he violate any of the six elementary rules for good writing that Orwell prescribes? Where? Is his style complex because his subject and thought require it, or is he merely indulging in ornate diction?

4. In his first paragraph Mr. Tawney rules out liberty in a society where there are both servants and masters. Later he implies the acceptance of hierarchy so long as those at the top can be called to account. Can these two views be reconciled?

5. What are Mr. Tawney's principal strictures on the society that had followed most of Adam Smith's advice? To what extent are they theoretical, to what extent based on experience or observation?

6. When Mr. Tawney says the nation applauds an idea "with self-congratulatory gestures of decorous enthusiasm," is he employing elegant ridicule, or what?

7. If his central aim is further reform in Britain, why does he turn to the United States for his chief example of economic tyranny?

8. Does he indicate what served to domesticate "the creature" in Britain? Couldn't what remains to be done be left to the same social forces to effect?

9. What is implied in his likening of the industrial baron to a prehistoric monster?

10. Mr. Lasswell spoke of "symbols of the common destiny" as the elite's ideology, the counter-elite's Utopia. Do you find any such symbols here? What are they? What purpose do they serve?

DE TOCQUEVILLE: Tyranny of the Majority

1. How valid and pertinent do de Tocqueville's remarks seem today? If you were writing on the power of the majority in government, wouldn't you have to examine the defensive weapons and tactics that are available to minorities in the United States?

2. To justify his defiance of an unjust law, de Tocqueville says he would appeal to "the sovereignty of mankind." How could he defend the statement if asked for particulars? Why should he employ the appeal of the conventional revolutionary?

3. Try your hand at a dialogue between Socrates and Tocqueville on democracy.

4. De Tocqueville states that there is more freedom of speech in every country in Europe than in the United States. If you accept that at face value for the 1830's, would you think it true or false for the 1960's? What sort of evidence would you need to support your answer?

5. Can you relate Tocqueville's remarks in his final paragraph to the current debate over conformity, "the organization man," and the homogenization of our culture?

6. If the author were to return and write a preface for a new edition of his work, what remark might be made about David Riesman's *The Lonely Crowd*?

HAND: The Meaning of Liberty

1. In the first paragraph Judge Hand explains why he tried to avoid talking on liberty, and what made him do it. What is the purpose of these introductory remarks? Do they increase your curiosity about what is to come or give life to the subject?

2. Can you trace the stages of his journey from an initial negative reaction through to his "very small quarry?" How does he manage the transition from one stage to the next?

3. What is the outcome of his search for an objective standard for the content of liberty? Is he on the side of the "cultivated snob" or his opponent? Or is he saying that there is no yardstick for good and evil, whether in Athens or in Nazi Germany? Would his own final good be within reach in either?

4. In the penultimate paragraph Judge Hand suddenly jumps from the ant to the ape. Could you devise a transition sentence that would bring in his "simian cousins" less abruptly?

5. Judge Hand's ideal society permits "free and spontaneous meddling." In view of the unpleasant connotation of "meddle" could he have put this another way?

6. Is he implying in the final paragraph that whoever accepts faith "in the indefectible significance" of the individual is obligated to be himself at whatever cost? What is the relation of this faith to liberty?

CHURCHILL: Address to Congress

1. What was Churchill's primary aim in addressing Congress? What means did he employ to achieve it? Is his an appeal to reason, to interest, to emotion? How much of the speech could be labelled blandishment, exhortation, information, morale-building?

2. Churchill's eloquence has become proverbial. The Oxford Dictionary defines eloquence as "fluency, force and appropriateness." Sir Herbert Read lists as necessary conditions "an adequate theme," "a sincere and impassioned mind," and "a power of sustainment or pertinacity." Does Churchill's address to Congress meet these specifications? Does it in any way illustrate the rhetorical weaknesses Read found in his pre-war writing (mentioned in the headnote)?

3. List all the ways Churchill alludes to Anglo-American solidarity as natural and advantageous (aside from his parentage), not only for the duration but on into the future.

4. Can you make any general statements about what Congress will laugh at or applaud by an analysis of what precedes each indication of audience response?

5. After noting the adjectives Churchill applied to Germany and Japan, and the small space devoted to the enemy countries, would you say there was any degree of war-mongering or invective in the address? What motive does he appeal to in the interest of our combined and unstinted war effort?

WHITTEMORE: Churchill as a Mythmaker

1. Can you put in a few words the nature of Mr. Whittemore's initial doubts about Churchill and what then convinced him that Churchill deserved his respect and qualified admiration?

2. What do the "limitations of myth" turn out to be?

3. Mr. Whittemore is convinced that Churchill thought by writing, revising, re-writing. You may recall that Orwell advised you to begin your thinking without using words lest the words derail the thought. The question about Churchill which we cannot answer is whether, while his successive revisions gained in eloquence, they drifted away from the event he was narrating and commenting on.

4. Does Mr. Whittemore meet the requirement of live metaphors and fresh

phrases? Is his humor detached or integrated with the line of thought? How would you characterize it?

5. How has your own estimate of Churchill changed in the course of reading this essay?

CONNOLLY and GLASS: The Censure of Senator Nye

1. Compare the modes of denunciation employed by Senators Connolly and Glass. Do you find satire, ridicule, outright sarcasm (which comes from a verb meaning "to tear flesh")? Which approach do you think was more effective?

2. Both Senators say they are constrained from saying what they would like. How seriously is this to be taken? How does Senator Glass leap the barrier of the impermissible?

3. Both Senators agree that their colleague was a coward. What is the old American base for this charge? How applicable is it in this instance?

4. Is Senator Connolly's figure of Pike's Peak towering over the Arkansas bog any more or less effective for being geographically absurd?

5. What is the significance of the fact that neither Senator went into the question of whether President Wilson had in fact made contradictory statements about his knowledge of the secret treaties?

MORSE: The Verbiage of Defense and Attack

1. When a Senator is maligned, either by a colleague or by a rash journalist, he has one of two options. He might disdain to reply at all, but how would his silence be interpreted? The customary response is a speech in which the offender is denounced as mendacious and untrustworthy, without credentials in his own profession or status as a gentleman. How well does Senator Morse follow the formula? What does he add to it? How does his treatment of Dirksen compare with his treatment of Alsop?

2. A political party of the 1850's, labelled Know-nothings, made capital of the American dislike of recent immigrants. Is there any appropriateness in using the same name for opponents of foreign aid? Even if not, hasn't the term some cutting power?

RUSSELL and DOUGLAS: The Pros and Cons of Civil Rights

1. Senator Russell and Senator Douglas both indicate their devotion to equality. Is the real issue between them property rights, the President's appeal to the nation and Congress, "mingling of the races," or what?

2. In concentrating on the accommodations provisions of the civil rights proposals, Senator Russell chose an issue that found the North divided. By

what means is he able to equate this feature of civil rights for Negroes with socialism? How important is this in his argument?

3. In his remarks on the "tortured commerce clause," Senator Russell uses the "opening wedge" argument: if you integrate restaurants under that clause, no citizen's living room or bedroom will be safe. Isn't there a shift here from commercial to non-commercial? If the opening wedge argument depends on its plausibility or credibility, is this use of the device effective?

4. Senator Douglas' pessimism about civil rights legislation was confirmed by the adjournment of Congress six months later with a bill still in committee. What was the basis of his gloomy forecast? What gave him a measure of hope?

5. Does either Senator say anything to win converts, or is each talking to himself and his friends? Do you find them equally eloquent, persuasive, logical, informative, inspiring?

KING: I Have a Dream

1. This speech can be classed as a manifesto. To whom is it addressed, and what is its central purpose?

2. James Reston of the *New York Times* wrote that Dr. King's address was an "anguished echo" from all the old American reformers: Roger Williams, Sam Adams, Thoreau, William Lloyd Garrison, Eugene V. Debs. Can you identify passages reminiscent of each of them? What is not an echo?

3. King was said to be "both militant and sad" and his voice "melodious and melancholy." Can you inject these qualities into your silent reading of the speech, or must it be read aloud?

4. Do any of King's figures of speech and cadences strike you as Biblical? Do any come out of the American articles of faith?

5. Are there times when figures of speech should not be newly coined, but taken from the old mint? How does the phrase "solid rock of brotherhood" fit with your answer?

LINCOLN: With Malice Toward None

1. What is Lincoln's main purpose? Is he addressing more than one audience?

2. Do you find instances of balance in the address? Do any suggest opposition as between the two warring antagonists? Are any merely rhetorical embellishments?

3. Lincoln's words, hallowed though they are, need not be read uncritically. Does he violate any of Orwell's precepts for economical, expressive prose? Consider this sentence: "Neither side expected for the war the magnitude or the duration which it has already attained." Could that be said as eloquently but more directly in other words? How?

4. Though he attaches war-guilt to the South in the second paragraph, doesn't Lincoln virtually withdraw the charge and even offer to share the guilt by the end of the following paragraph? Why?

5. Examine the rhetorical tactics Lincoln employs in the long complex sentence which begins, "If we shall suppose that American slavery. . . ." "If we shall suppose . . ." has all the appearance of a conditional clause, but it has no bearing on the final question to which there is only one answer. Is such a coercive tactic justified? When is it fair and when not?

6. Discuss the aim, message and tone of the fine peroration. Orators generally end their speeches with passages of particular eloquence. Is Lincoln's purpose the usual one?

KENNEDY: Inaugural Address

1. Lincoln's inaugural was wholly devoted to the subject of the Civil War. Kennedy's also has a single major theme. What is it? You might check your answer by counting the words ("symbols of our common heritage") and note which occur most frequently. You may discover by this means a minor theme.

2. How does Kennedy link the present with the past, and for what purpose?

3. How many times in the address is the antithesis between friend and foe mentioned or suggested? The central dilemma of the Cold War is stated in the paragraph beginning "But neither can two great and powerful groups." Can you think of any more exact or eloquent way to say it? What is proposed as a means of easing and finally terminating the Cold War?

4. What is the significance of stating that a new generation of Americans has come into power?

5. How many of the key words might be termed inspirational or exhortative? Could the entire address be called an exhortation? Is there anyone to whom it is not addressed in whole or part?

RESTON: Uniquack Explains de Gaulle

1. What is Mr. Reston's purpose in this essay? Is he trying to illuminate problems of the Western alliance? When he satirizes politicians does he expect any change in them or their successors? Could he be mixing entertainment with home truths as he sees them?

2. Does the device of Uniquack enable the writer to speak more freely, irresponsibly, emphatically? Can you characterize the questioner by his comments on Uniquack's pronouncements? Is either Mr. Reston?

3. The paragraph about Mr. Khrushchev is ironic and satirical. What is the irony, and who is being satirized?

4. Did you read Uniquack's statements with enough suspicion to be unusually alert to irony?

5. What do you make of the statement that de Gaulle cannot forgive us and the British for the favors we have done him?

BUCHWALD: Congressional Featherbedding

1. How should Art Buchwald's essay be judged? In reading it into the *Congressional Record,* Senator Clark described Buchwald as entertaining and humorous and then said approvingly that he had ridiculed Congress "with biting satire." Do you agree that the satire is "biting?" If not, what adjectives would you think more precise?

2. Finley Peter Dunne once said he was saved from mayhem at the hands of his victims by employing humor and Mr. Dooley's Irish brogue. Here Mr. Buchwald charges Congressmen with featherbedding, absenteeism, headline-seeking, etc. What saved him from Congressional castigation? Was he playing safe by making no mention of the filibuster and the veto power of the eldest statesmen? Would he have been in trouble if he had substituted for the non-sensical heading he used "Congress is a Fraud?"

3. Has the writer in this piece any purpose beyond earning his living and giving us entertainment? Why did two reformist Senators want his essay in the record?

4. Mark any passages that earn a laugh. What are the devices that the humorist uses, and which are most effective? To what extent does Mr. Buchwald rely on incongruity, word-play, surprise, exaggeration?

COUSINS: Modern Man Is Obsolete

1. Writing in 1945 Mr. Cousins said that two courses were open to man in the Atomic Age. Can you state them in single sentences, in single words? What was the author's attitude toward the second course? Why did he offer it as an alternative? Does the violence in it connote more than the murder and destruction it prescribes?

2. What course has man in fact pursued since 1945? Why didn't Mr. Cousins include it as a third choice? Do you think he overlooked this possibility, or deliberately limited his alternatives to two, one good, one bad, to force readers to accept the right one? Is there any logical necessity for limiting alternatives to two?

3. Mr. Cousins frequently refers to fear and says man will always fear when he can find no answer. How does the writer himself employ fear in support of his answer? How does he justify the use of fear to back a rational program?

4. In the new age Mr. Cousins finds everything covered by a blanket of obsolescence (Para. 4). Why did he include poetry? To signify the blanket's infinite spread? Because it alliterates with politics?

5. George Orwell warned against foreign words and long words derived

from the ancient languages. Should Mr. Cousins be reproved for fearing that the birth certificate of the Atomic Age will be its *memento mori?* What could Mr. Orwell do with the sentence: ". . . modern man is obsolete, a self-made anachronism becoming more incongruous by the minute"?

6. What are the tactics of persuasion used in this argument?

7. How does the author view an age? Is it merely a stage? Can it be characterized by a single word, such as Stone Age, Atomic Age? If so, could you expect to find everything in it in harmony with its most conspicuous characteristics?

Does a new age die by being born (like the new year)? What does the death of the old imply? You may like the figure of speech which has man stumbling over the threshold of the new age. This implies that the door has been unlocked and stands open. Can you think of other ways to signify the beginning of a new age?

8. The writer repeatedly states that man *must* bring himself up to date, but is there any evidence in the essay that man *can?*

9. Once Mr. Cousins speaks of building on soapbubbles. What is suggested by the figure beyond insubstantiality?

10. Note the many references to time, stated in periods and speed of time, implied in "obsolete." Do you think the author saw any incongruity between the long time spans he mentions and his demand that a complete transformation be achieved overnight?

2   3   4   5   6   7   8   9   0